Buzz

DK

LONDON, NEW YORK, MUNICH,
MELBOURNE, and DELHI

Written and edited by Caroline Bingham,
Ben Morgan, Matthew Robertson
Designers Tory Gordon-Harris, Karen Hood
Editorial assistance Fleur Star
Design assistants Gemma Fletcher, Sadie Thomas
DTP designer Ben Hung
Illustrator Mark Beech
Production Claire Pearson
Picture research Liz Moore
Jacket designer Hedi Gutt

Publishing manager Susan Leonard
Art director Rachael Foster

Category publisher Mary Ling
Creative director Jane Bull

Consultant Matthew Robertson

First published in the United States by
DK Publishing
375 Hudson Street
New York, New York 10014

07 08 09 10 10 9 8 7 6 5 4 3 2 1

A catalog record for this book is available from the Library of Congress.

ISBN 978-0-7566-2912-0
BD322 04/07

Color reproduction by Wyndeham-Icon, London
Printed and bound by Hung Hing Printing Company, China

Discover more at **www.dk.com**

What's all the *buzz*

Socialize with sociable ants, bees, and termites starting on **page 90**

Am I a moth or a butterfly? Find out on **page 60**

All arachnids are available at **page 106**

Fly to **page 80** for freaky food facts

about these bugs?

Learn about beetles, from **page 46**

Follow a swarm of locusts on **page 76**

BUZZZ

Make a beeline to a beehive **page 96**

Am I a centipede or a millipede? **page 116**

400 million years ago (or thereabouts), the ancient ancestors of today's **insects**, **millipedes**, and **spiders** crawled out of the sea and set up home on land. They were the **FIRST ANIMALS** **ever** to walk on land. Another 399 million years were to pass before **humans** arrived. If all the world's humans and *all other* large animals were to disappear, the tiny creepy crawlies that share our planet would carry on with life without a second thought.

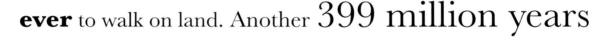

But if *they* disappeared, our world would collapse. With no bees and bugs to pollinate **flowers**, crops would fail and we would **starve.** With **NO** beetles and flies to recycle our waste, dead bodies and *dung* would pile up all over the place. The little creatures that **crawl** around our gardens, **creep** across our ceilings, and **buzz** around our lives are MORE than *important.* **They are** essential. Without them, the world would be a very **nasty** place indeed.

ARTHROPOD

= "jointed foot"

Insects, **spiders**, and other *creepy-crawlies* make up a **family** of animals known as THE **ARTHROPODS**. The word *arthropod* means "**jointed foot**," and that's what all these **animals** have: tiny legs made of stiff little **struts** joined together like *model toys*.

Black widow spider

Arthropods can also have...

- two brains (one for seeing and one for eating)
- blood that looks green
- ears on their knees
- tasters on their feet
- lifespans from just a few weeks to 30 years
- bodies as small as a grain of salt or as big as a shark (... fortunately that one is extinct!)

Ladybug

The most **important** feature that *all arthropods* share is this: THEIR BODIES ARE INSIDE OUT. Most big animals, such as cats and dogs and human beings, have a **skeleton** on the inside. An arthropod's is ***on the outside***. Like a suit of armor, the external skeleton (or *exoskeleton*) is made of stiff plates linked together. Between the plates are flexible joints that let the body move.

The **exoskeleton** is the secret of the arthropods' **success** because it's so adaptable. Different bits of it have evolved into all kinds of different structures, from claws and jaws to wings and stings. But there's a catch. External skeletons can't **stretch**, so arthropods have to shed them and make new ones in order to grow bigger.

Hoverfly

Flower beetle

7

Long legs, short legs, fat legs, thin legs, hairy legs, smooth legs, prickly legs, soft legs, stron

HOW MANY

6

6 legs
—probably an insect. Insects are the most successful land animals on Earth. Most have six legs, a pair of feelers (antennae) at the front, two pairs of wings, and a body divided into three segments: a head, a thorax (chest), and an abdomen (belly).

8

8 legs
—probably an arachnid. Spiders, scorpions, ticks, and mites are all arachnids. Unlike insects, arachnids never have wings or antennae, and their bodies are divided into only two segments. Most of them are flesh eaters.

10

LEGS?

There are millions of different arthropods, so how do you tell them apart? Here's a clue: *count the legs*. Most arthropods belong to one of four major categories, and the number of legs is a good clue to the right category.

10 legs
—probably a crustacean. Crabs, lobsters, crayfish, and shrimp are all crustaceans. Most crustaceans live in water and breathe through gills. Not all have 10 legs, though—they can have dozens or none at all. Woodlice are crustaceans that live on land, and they have 14 legs each.

Loads of legs
—probably a centipede or a millipede. These arthropods have long thin bodies divided into lots of segments, with legs on each segment. *Centipede* means "a hundred feet" and *millipede* means "a thousand feet," but, in fact, the number of feet can be anything from 30 to 750.

0 legs

No legs
—probably a slug or a snail or a worm. These slippery creatures **aren't arthropods**. They have no jointed legs and no external skeleton. Slugs and snails do have feet though, but only one—a single giant foot all the way along the body.

30+

The branches on this tree show how closely related different types of arthropod are. Termites and cockroaches are close relatives, so they sit on closely connected branches. In contrast, centipedes and millipedes are actually distant relatives and so have long branches of their own.

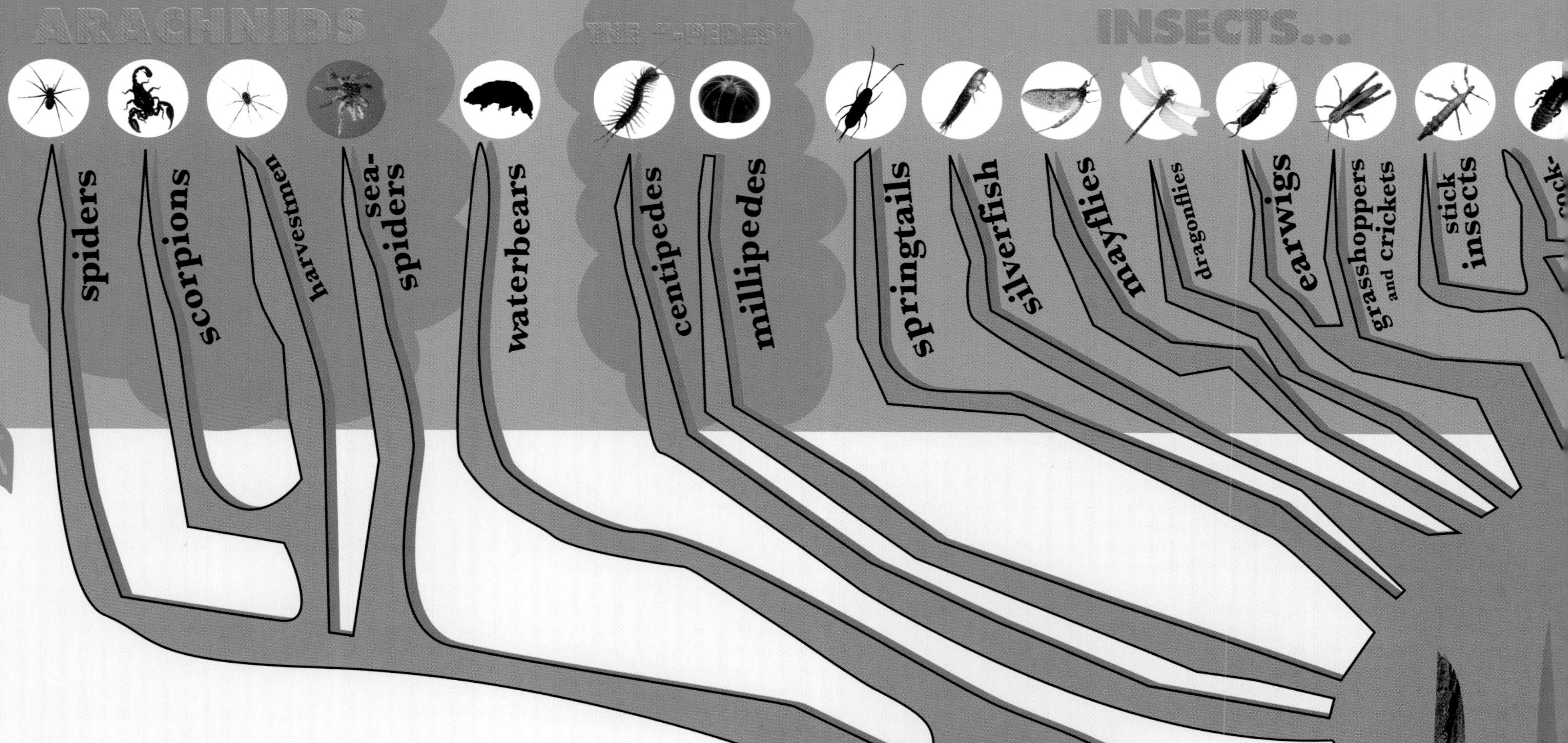

ARACHNIDS
THE "-PEDES"
INSECTS...
spiders
scorpions
harvestmen
sea-spiders
waterbears
centipedes
millipedes
springtails
silverfish
mayflies
dragonflies
earwigs
grasshoppers and crickets
stick insects
cock-

Arthropods evolved from worms about half a billion years ago. Since then, thousands of different varieties have evolved. This family tree shows how the four main categories (arachnids, the "-pedes," insects, and crustaceans) evolved into dozens of different branches. In reality, each small branch at the top should have millions of twigs (one twig for each species) but there wouldn't be room for every species even if this page were ten thousand times bigger.

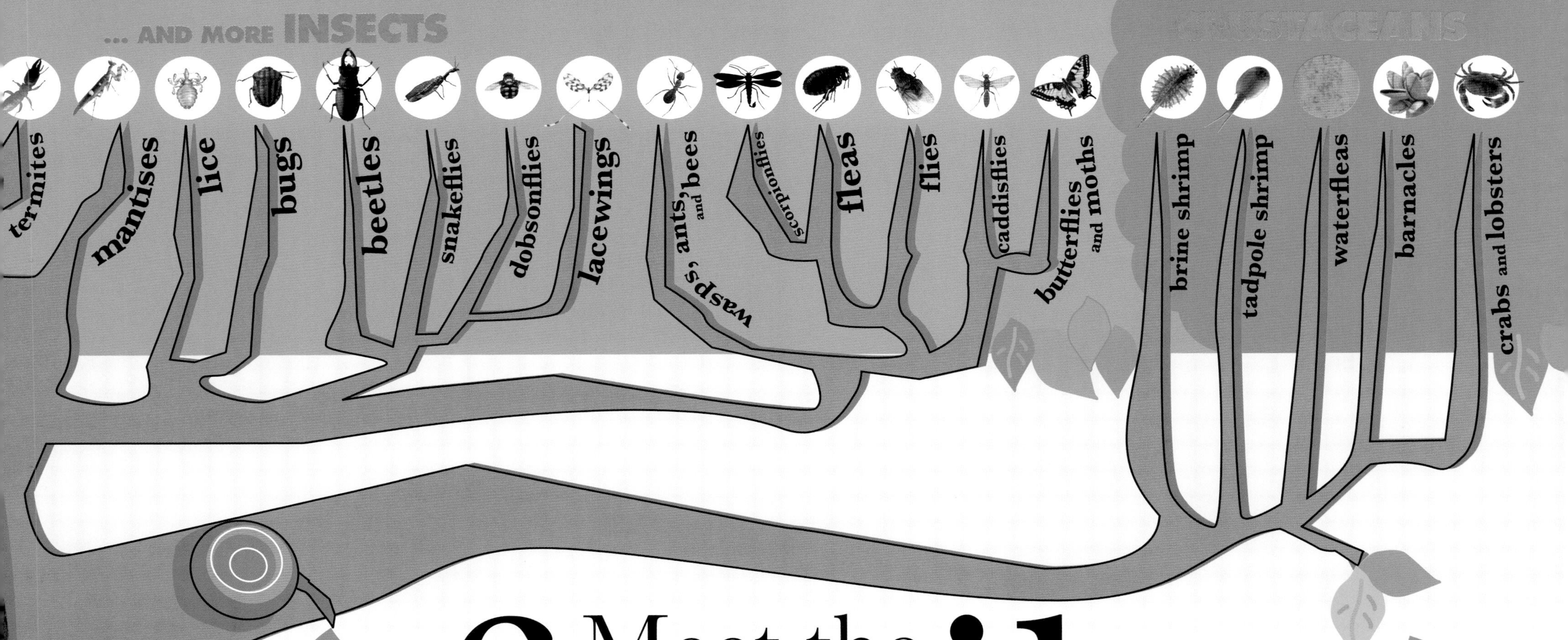
... AND MORE INSECTS
CRUSTACEANS
termites
mantises
lice
bugs
beetles
snakeflies
dobsonflies
lacewings
wasps, ants, and bees
scorpionflies
fleas
flies
caddisflies
butterflies and moths
brine shrimp
tadpole shrimp
waterfleas
barnacles
crabs and lobsters

Meet the family

WHO RULES THE WORLD?

If you shared out the world's land by number of species, arthropods would get every continent and island except South America.

At least **90%**

of animal species on Earth are **ARTHROPODS**

Arthropods are the most successful animals on Earth. They've conquered *land, sea,* and *air* and live everywhere from the depths of the oceans to the tops of mountains. Scientists have so far discovered and named about 1.2 million different types, or species, of animal. About 9 out of 10 of these—more than a million in total—are arthropods.

But those are just the species that have been cataloged. There are **countless more** waiting to be discovered. Around 25 new arthropod species are discovered **every day,** and there's currently a 15-year backlog of newly discovered species waiting to be officially named and described. So the true number of arthropod species alive is anybody's guess, but it's probably **millions**.

Insects are the **biggest** group of arthropods by far, with more than 900,000 named species. According to one expert, the total number of *individual* insects alive on Earth is 120 million billion. In other words...

for **every person** alive today, there are *200 million* insects.

13

How arthropods conquered

520 MYA

Within a few million years, arthropods were scuttling all over the seafloor like huge woodlice. These were **trilobites**—the most successful animals of their day. They ruled the seas for nearly 300 million years. Their tough skeletons formed millions of fossils that are easy to find even today.

540 MYA

Our story starts 540 million years ago (MYA), when there was little life on Earth besides microbes and worms on the seabed. Some of the worms evolved external skeletons, and their segments sprouted legs—they became **arthropods**. Soon, these new creatures would conquer the world.

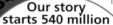

505 MYA

Millions of years before sharks evolved, arthropods were the top predators in the sea. The trilobites' number one enemy was probably *Anomalocaris*, a monstrous, shrimplike creature that was bigger than a man and had gigantic claws at the front for snatching trilobites. It was the great white shark of its day.

Prehistoric arthropods grew to gigantic sizes. The biggest were probably *Eurypterids*—scorpionlike sea creatures that reached 13 ft (4 m) long (as big as a crocodile). Their tails were tipped with a vicious spike that may have been used to inject venom.

438–408 MYA

428 MYA

428 million years ago, arthropods began to conquer the land. **Millipedes** about ½ in (1 cm) long became the first animals ever to walk on our planet.

350 MYA

By 350 million years ago, land arthropods had evolved into giants, too. Millipedes grew to 7 ft (2 m) long and scorpions were 3 ft (1 m) long—as big as a dog.

320 MYA

The **first ever flying animals** were insects. They looked like a cross between mayflies and cockroaches and had either four or six beautifully patterned wings. Insects remained the only flying animals on Earth until 100 million years later, when pterosaurs evolved.

300 MYA

Lush **forests** spread across the land during the Carboniferous Period. Towering trees provided new habitats for animals, but only for those that could reach them. So having conquered land and sea, the arthropods took to the air…

Silverfish—slithering silvery insects with no wings—appeared 300 million years ago and have barely changed since.

PRECAMBRIAN **CAMBRIAN** **ORDOVICIAN** **SILURIAN** **DEVONIAN** **CARBONIFEROUS**

600 million years ago (MYA) **500** **400** **300**

the world...

280 MYA
By 280 million years ago, even the flying insects had become giants. The skies were ruled by dragonfly-like creatures called **griffenflies**, which swooped about on 30 in (75 cm) wingspans.

1ST IN THE AIR

220–209 MYA
Wasps appeared in the late Triassic Period. The first wasps were small, solitary insects. Later on, wasps began to form colonies.

140 MYA
The first fleas probably sucked the blood of dinosaurs. Later on they adapted to live off of birds and mammals as well.

How do we know?

Everything we know about the history of arthropods comes from fossils—the remains of ancient animals preserved in rock. The best insect fossils are found in amber, a honey-colored rock formed from the sticky sap of pine trees. Even insects trapped in amber 100 million years ago look as if they died only yesterday, with legs and wings perfectly intact. Thanks to amber, we know that all the main types of insect were here on Earth 90 million years ago.

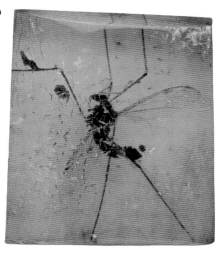

40-million-year-old fossilized fly in amber

230 MYA
Beetles appeared in the Triassic, after the first dinosaurs.

Dinosaurs first appeared about now.

201–185 MYA
Moths appeared in the early Jurassic Period.

145–133 MYA
Ants appeared about 140 million years ago. They evolved from social wasps that had given up flying.

92–73 MYA
Butterflies appeared in the late Cretaceous. They evolved from moths.

PERMIAN **TRIASSIC** **JURASSIC** **CRETACEOUS** **CENOZOIC**

200 **100** **NOW**

Besides the insects and spiders we see around us, there are billions more too tiny to notice. Most of these are mites and springtails, which live in soil and among rotting leaves, where they graze on fungi and microbes. Just 1 sq yd (1 m²) of an average forest floor can contain up to 1.5 million of these tiny arthropods. So every time you take a step, your shoe covers more than 20,000 of them!

1 yd (1 m)

1 yd (1 m)

700,000 springtails

70 ants

50 woodlice

5,000 harvestmen

1 SQUARE YARD OF LAND?

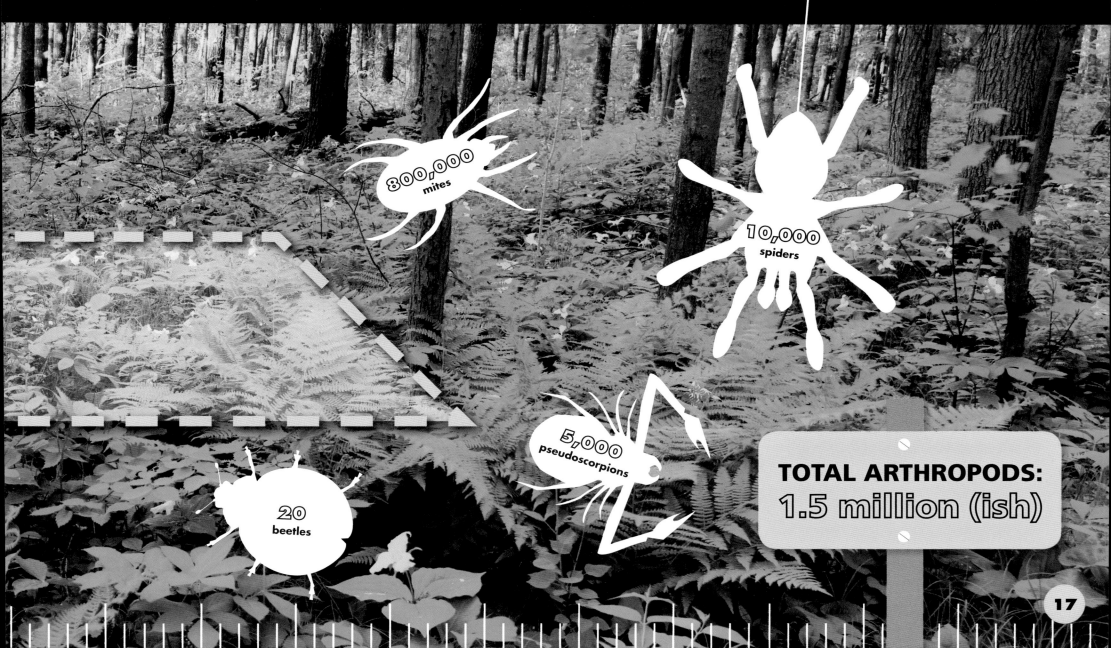

800,000
mites

10,000
spiders

5,000
pseudoscorpions

20
beetles

TOTAL ARTHROPODS:
1.5 million (ish)

17

What is an insect?

Hoverfly

Insects are the most successful and common of all the arthropods. In fact, they are so common that lots of people say "insect" when they actually mean "arthropod." The secret of the insects' success was the invention of flight, which allowed the very earliest insects to flee from enemies and conquer new habitats. Today's insects all share certain key features that were passed down from those distant ancestors. Typically, adult insects have 6 legs, 2 pairs of wings, and a body divided into 3 main zones: the head, the thorax (chest), and the abdomen (belly).

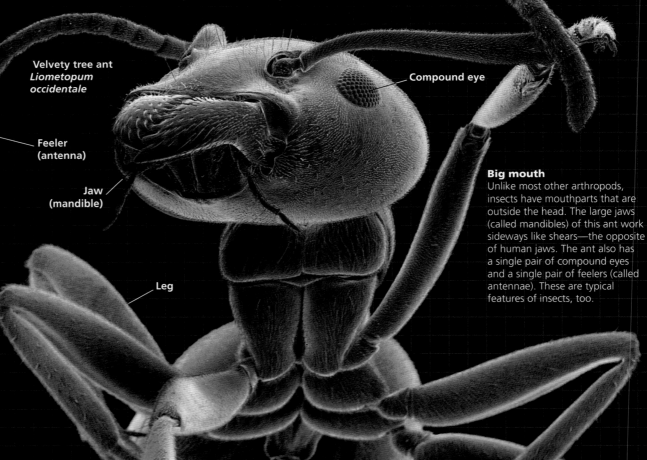

Velvety tree ant
Liometopum occidentale

Feeler (antenna)

Jaw (mandible)

Compound eye

Leg

Big mouth
Unlike most other arthropods, insects have mouthparts that are outside the head. The large jaws (called mandibles) of this ant work sideways like shears—the opposite of human jaws. The ant also has a single pair of compound eyes and a single pair of feelers (called antennae). These are typical features of insects, too.

Walking
Insects typically walk by moving three legs forward at once, then the other three, and so on. As a result, there are always at least three toes touching the ground at once, forming a triangle—the most stable type of shape. Six is the minimum number of legs needed to keep arthropod bodies stable, but the arrangement works so well that it is copied in robots.

Head

As with most animals, an insect's head is where the main sense organs, mouth, and brain are. The antennae not only feel objects but smell and taste them, too. The compound eyes are made of hundreds of separate eyes packed together.

Thorax

The thorax is where all the legs and wings attach. Inside it are powerful flight muscles. Most insects have two pairs of wings that beat together, but dragonflies beat theirs alternately. Flies use only one pair of wings, giving superb maneuverability —they can fly backward or even upside down.

Abdomen

The back end of an insect contains the main parts of its digestive system, the heart (which is tube-shaped), and sex organs. Some female insects have an egg-laying tube at the rear; in bees and wasps this tube is also the sting. There are no true legs on the abdomen, but caterpillar abdomens have false legs.

Flight muscles
In some insects the flight muscles pull on the base of the wings, but in others, such as this wasp, they pull on the wall of the thorax. This gives a faster wing beat.

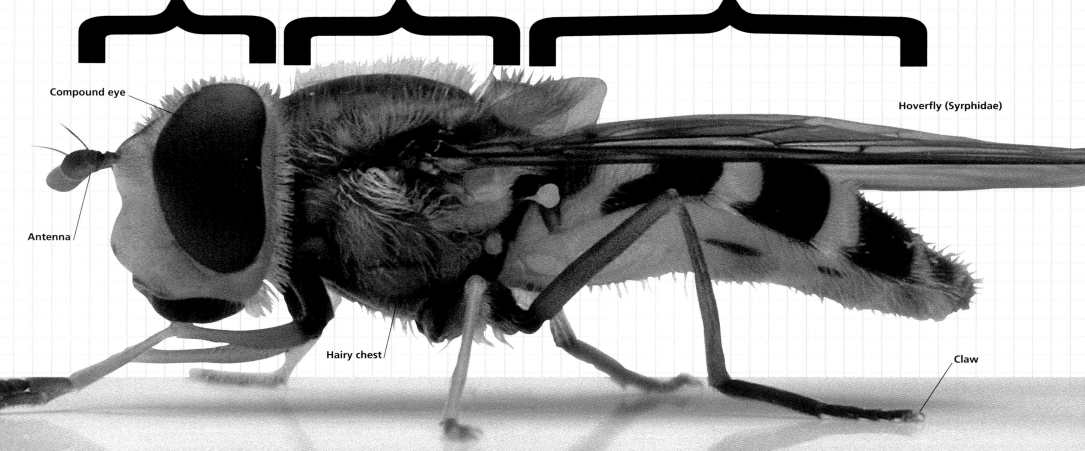

Compound eye

Antenna

Hairy chest

Hoverfly (Syrphidae)

Claw

Seen close-up, many insects are surprisingly hairy. The hairs help keep the flight muscles warm. Hairs on the legs also double as sense organs that can taste whatever they touch.

WINGS & THINGS

Insect wings are hugely important, both to insects and to people. Why? They help *insects* to escape, find food, and find and attract a mate. They help *people* to separate different insects into groups.

Vein

Membrane

Let's
LOOK at a **wing**

All insect wings are made up of thin membranes supported by a network of tiny veins. However, there are so many differences between different types of insect wings that entomologists use these differences to name some groups of winged insects.

THAT'S AMAZING!

Hoverflies beat their wings up to 1,000 times per second! They can also hover (a feat not many insects can achieve).

What *kind* of **wing**?

The Latin word ***pteron*** means "fur," "wing," or "feather." When used for insects, it means "wing." There are lots of insect groups, but some of the largest are the **Coleoptera**, or "sheath-winged" insects, the **Hymenoptera**, or "membranous-winged" insects, the **Diptera**, or "two-winged" insects, and the **Lepidoptera**, or "scale-winged" insects. Then there are the **Orthoptera**, with "straight wings," and the **Neuroptera** with their "nerve wings," the **Plecoptera**…

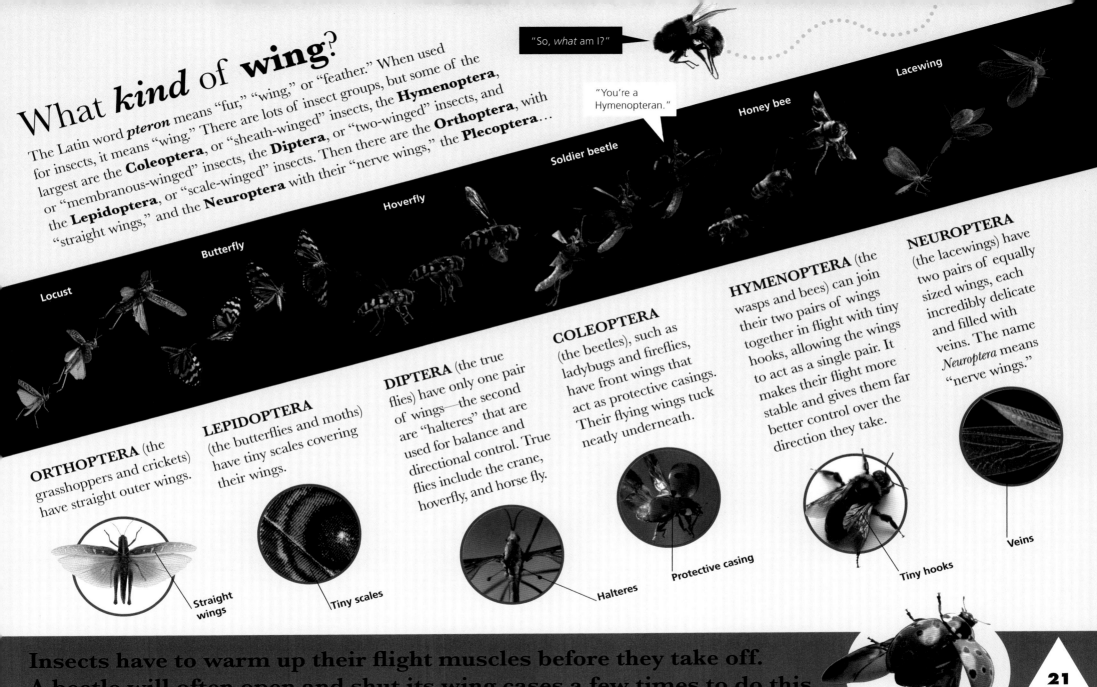

"So, *what* am I?"

"You're a Hymenopteran."

Lacewing

Honey bee

Soldier beetle

Hoverfly

Butterfly

Locust

NEUROPTERA (the lacewings) have two pairs of equally sized wings, each incredibly delicate and filled with veins. The name *Neuroptera* means "nerve wings."

HYMENOPTERA (the wasps and bees) can join their two pairs of wings together in flight with tiny hooks, allowing the wings to act as a single pair. It makes their flight more stable and gives them far better control over the direction they take.

COLEOPTERA (the beetles), such as ladybugs and fireflies, have front wings that act as protective casings. Their flying wings tuck neatly underneath.

DIPTERA (the true flies) have only one pair of wings—the second are "halteres" that are used for balance and directional control. True flies include the crane, hoverfly, and horse fly.

LEPIDOPTERA (the butterflies and moths) have tiny scales covering their wings.

ORTHOPTERA (the grasshoppers and crickets) have straight outer wings.

Straight wings

Tiny scales

Halteres

Protective casing

Tiny hooks

Veins

Insects have to warm up their flight muscles before they take off. A beetle will often open and shut its wing cases a few times to do this.

If you were an **insect**, what would **you** be**?**

Friendly?

DO YOU enjoy company (lots of it!)? Do you like to **travel**? Are you **hard-working**? Will you clean, build, feed lots of babies, and then collect food?

Looking good!

DO YOU like to look good? Are you at your best when you are the center of attention? Do you like to **dazzle** in bright, shiny colors?

Patient

ARE YOU prepared to wait a **long** time to get what you want? Do you like your own company? Can you move **fast** if necessary?

Singer?

DO YOU like singing? Have you got a **voice** that could be heard from some distance away? Do other people like to **hear** you sing?

PRAYING MANTISES
look motionless but take less than a second to strike.

ANTS
Some ants are able to lift objects many times their weight.

JEWEL BEETLES
have casings as shiny as precious gems.

WATER BOATMEN
are able to "walk" under the surface of a pond.

22

Try a simple quiz to find out!

Strong?

ARE YOU brave? Are you strong? Would you be able to **lift** something that weighed more than you and **carry** it on a long trip?

A night owl?

DO YOU light up a room with your personality? Do you like to stay up **late**? Are you good at communicating **without** sound?

Sporty?

DO YOU like sports? How would you like to spend a day **skimming** around the surface of a pond or lake on a rowboat *upside down*?

Neat?

ARE YOU a fussy eater, or will you try **anything**? Do you have good ball skills? Could you **roll** a ball bigger than you all day under the hot sun?

FIREFLIES
come out at night to communicate with flashes of light.

WORKER HONEYBEES
travel the equivalent of three trips around the Earth.

DUNG BEETLES
clear away oodles of dung. They also eat it!

CICADAS
produce the loudest of all insect calls.

IF YOU WERE AN INSECT...

... you would have **superhuman** abilities. You could walk up walls, lift huge weights, and leap hundreds of times your height. So what's the secret? Why are insects so fantastically strong? In fact, they aren't. Their amazing abilities are all down to how the **laws of physics** work if you're tiny. Imagine shrinking yourself to half your height. You wouldn't weigh half your normal weight, you'd weigh *eight times less*. If you halved your height again, you'd weigh *64 times less* than normal. Forces that involve weight, such as the force you need to lift things or jump, would be 64 times smaller too. So lifting and jumping would be shockingly easy. For insects, these forces are minuscule, so they seem to have superhuman strength. But not everything is quite so easy...

Although forces involving weight are tiny to insects, other forces can be overpowering. The sticky forces that hold water molecules together are much more noticeable to insects than to us. They give water a kind of skin that an insect can walk across. A single water droplet becomes a wobbly ball to climb over.

Dodging raindrops that are bigger than you is easy if you use the same technique as flies. They are light enough to let the tiny gust of air around each raindrop push them sideways, so they always miss the water. Even so, they avoid flying when it's pouring down!

Imagine being bombed by raindrops that weigh more than you do. This happens to insects all the time, but they simply bounce away without being hurt. The raindrops weigh so little that they don't carry enough force to cause an injury.

To protect against the sticky forces of water, insects have a water-repelling coat of wax on the body. Without this, a drop of water would be a deadly trap.

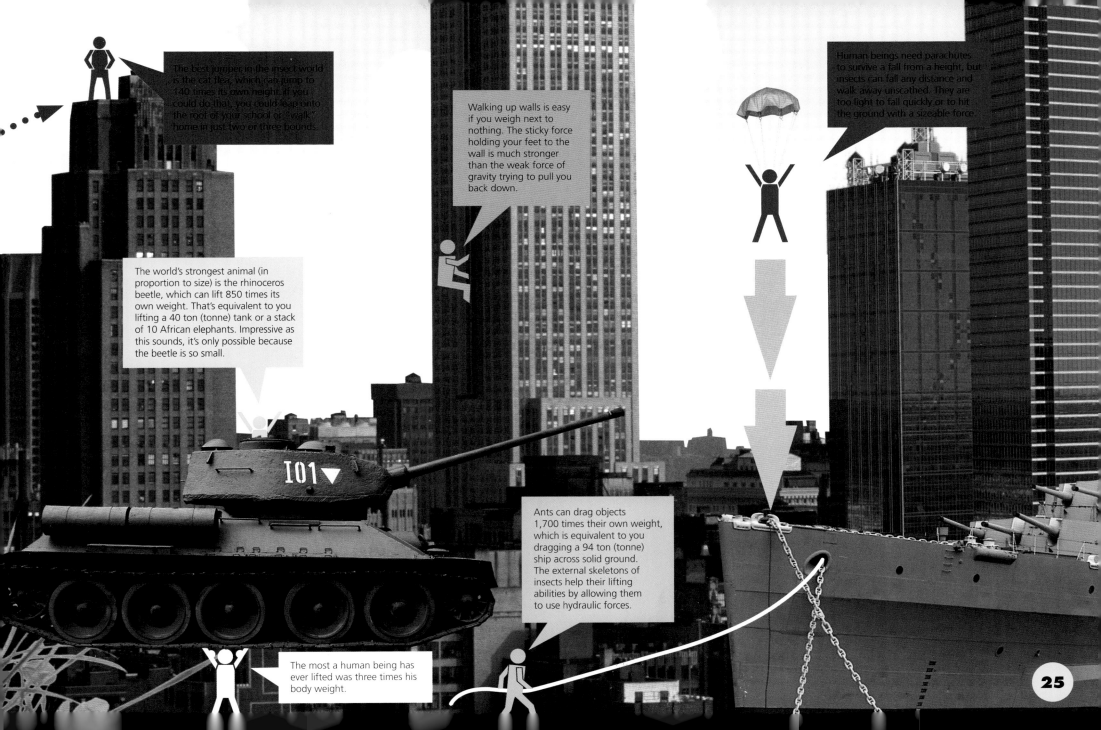

The best jumper in the insect world is the cat flea, which can jump to 140 times its own height. If you could do that, you could leap onto the roof of your school or "walk" home in just two or three bounds.

Walking up walls is easy if you weigh next to nothing. The sticky force holding your feet to the wall is much stronger than the weak force of gravity trying to pull you back down.

Human beings need parachutes to survive a fall from a height, but insects can fall any distance and walk away unscathed. They are too light to fall quickly or to hit the ground with a sizeable force.

The world's strongest animal (in proportion to size) is the rhinoceros beetle, which can lift 850 times its own weight. That's equivalent to you lifting a 40 ton (tonne) tank or a stack of 10 African elephants. Impressive as this sounds, it's only possible because the beetle is so small.

Ants can drag objects 1,700 times their own weight, which is equivalent to you dragging a 94 ton (tonne) ship across solid ground. The external skeletons of insects help their lifting abilities by allowing them to use hydraulic forces.

The most a human being has ever lifted was three times his body weight.

UPSIDE DOWN

Have you ever watched a fly or other insect walking up the wall and then along the ceiling? Don't you wish you could do that too? Just how do they manage to defeat the laws of gravity?

x 100

x 1,000

Did you know?
A housefly spends its life in the same area; they don't move far from their place of birth.

A housefly has two claws on the end of each foot. Under these are two sticky pads, each covered with minute hairs. The hairs produce a gluelike substance.

So a fly effectively "glues" itself to the ceiling. The claws help it to push its leg off the ceiling. (It is because of these sticky pads and its hairy legs that the housefly is a carrier of all kinds of nasty diseases and germs.)

So how does a fly LAND on the ceiling? The fly does not fly upside down. Just before it lands the fly stretches its front legs over its head to reach the surface. It then hauls its body around in a kind of somersault to bring the remaining four legs in contact with the ceiling. Touchdown!

What's inside an insect?

An insect's skeleton is on the outside of its body rather than the inside. If we looked inside our own bodies, we would find our organs surrounded and held together by our bones. So what happens inside an insect's body?

Let's look at a locust

Like people, insects have to eat, process food, breathe, carry blood, and sense the surrounding world with their organs. It's a lot to fit inside a tiny body!

Brainbox
The brain is the insect's control center. It lies behind the eye.

Stomach
An insect's stomach is called a crop. Food is slightly broken down in the stomach.

Heart
An insect's heart is at the center of its body. The heart pumps blood around the body.

Nervous system
Nerve centers are attached to the nerve cord. They send messages to the muscles.

Ganglion
A ganglion is a dense collection of nerve cells. Insects have several. This one controls the mouth.

Gizzard
In some insects, the gizzard grinds up the food a little more than the stomach does.

Ovaries
Fertilized eggs pass through an egg-laying tube and are laid in soft, damp soil.

28

Grasshoppers, crickets, and locusts are grouped in the same order of insects: Orthoptera. There are thousands of different species—at least 20,000 different grasshoppers and crickets alone. Below is just a small selection!

Locust

Grasshopper

Grasshopper

Grasshopper

Locust

Grasshopper

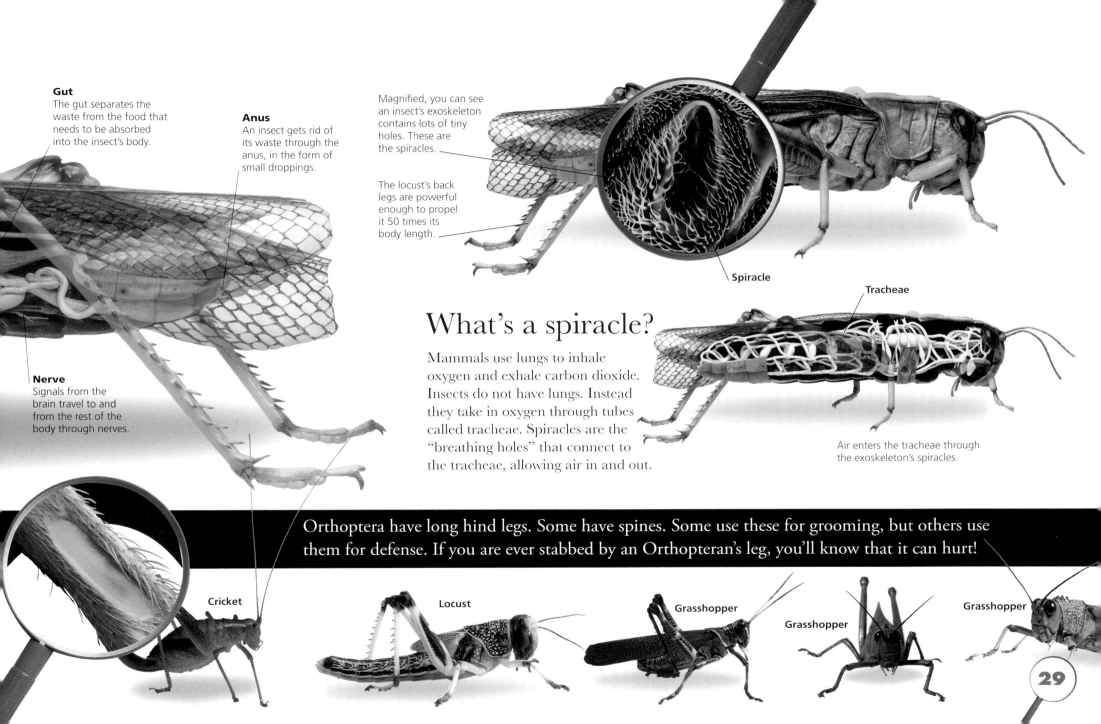

Gut
The gut separates the waste from the food that needs to be absorbed into the insect's body.

Anus
An insect gets rid of its waste through the anus, in the form of small droppings.

Magnified, you can see an insect's exoskeleton contains lots of tiny holes. These are the spiracles.

The locust's back legs are powerful enough to propel it 50 times its body length.

Spiracle

Tracheae

Nerve
Signals from the brain travel to and from the rest of the body through nerves.

What's a spiracle?

Mammals use lungs to inhale oxygen and exhale carbon dioxide. Insects do not have lungs. Instead they take in oxygen through tubes called tracheae. Spiracles are the "breathing holes" that connect to the tracheae, allowing air in and out.

Air enters the tracheae through the exoskeleton's spiracles.

Orthoptera have long hind legs. Some have spines. Some use these for grooming, but others use them for defense. If you are ever stabbed by an Orthopteran's leg, you'll know that it can hurt!

Cricket

Locust

Grasshopper

Grasshopper

Grasshopper

eye SEE things you *wouldn't believe!*

What big eyes you have!
Dragonflies have the largest compound eyes of all insects. Each eye is made up of 30,000 "facets".

How many eyes does an insect have?

Many insects have two eyes, but believe it or not, a lot of insects have five! A honeybee, for example, has two multisurface, compound eyes as well as three simple eyes (or "ocelli"). So do a grasshopper and a dragonfly. The simple eyes help these insects to detect light and movement. The compound eyes allow them to see the world in detail.

INSECTS DON'T HAVE EYELIDS. THEY RUB THEIR

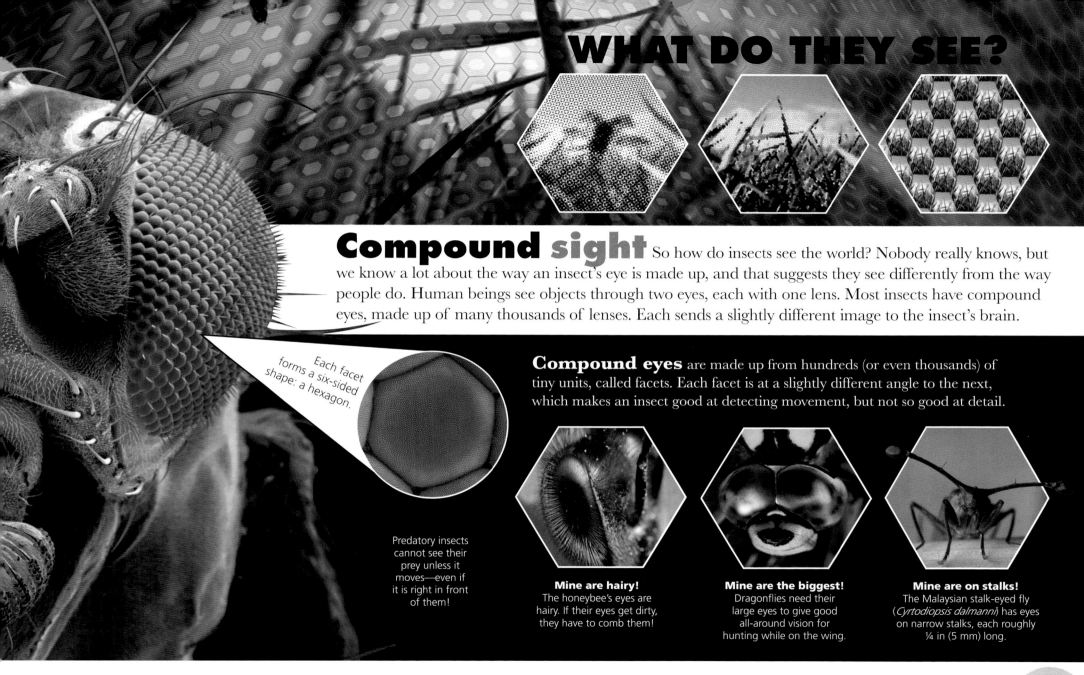

Compound sight

So how do insects see the world? Nobody really knows, but we know a lot about the way an insect's eye is made up, and that suggests they see differently from the way people do. Human beings see objects through two eyes, each with one lens. Most insects have compound eyes, made up of many thousands of lenses. Each sends a slightly different image to the insect's brain.

Each facet forms a six-sided shape: a hexagon.

Compound eyes are made up from hundreds (or even thousands) of tiny units, called facets. Each facet is at a slightly different angle to the next, which makes an insect good at detecting movement, but not so good at detail.

Predatory insects cannot see their prey unless it moves—even if it is right in front of them!

Mine are hairy!
The honeybee's eyes are hairy. If their eyes get dirty, they have to comb them!

Mine are the biggest!
Dragonflies need their large eyes to give good all-around vision for hunting while on the wing.

Mine are on stalks!
The Malaysian stalk-eyed fly (*Cyrtodiopsis dalmanni*) has eyes on narrow stalks, each roughly ¼ in (5 mm) long.

FORELIMBS ACROSS THEIR EYES TO KEEP THEM CLEAN.

LARGER than life!

Is it a beetle?

Weevils are a type of beetle. In fact, they form the largest group of beetles, with around 48,000 known members. This strikingly colorful weevil is the *Eupholus bennetti* from Papua New Guinea.

A troublesome insect

A weevil's long snout (its "rostrum") ends in tiny chewing mouthparts and it uses these well. Weevils are the cause of much damage to crops, especially since they eat all parts of a plant, from the leaves and flowers to the seeds and fruits.

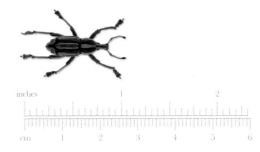

inches   1   2

cm   1   2   3   4   5   6

EUPHOLUS BENNETTI REACHES JUST OVER 1 IN (2.5 CM).

THE **HUNGER** BUG

Most people in the world will eat all kinds of **invertebrates** given the chance: perhaps you've tried *lobster, shrimp, oysters, crayfish, crab, or a particular shellfish*? They are all popular. Many people will happily **eat cooked insects and spiders** as well. There is actually little difference. The eating of insects even has a name: **ENTOMOPHAGY**.

BUGS FOR breakfast, lunch, *and dinner*. That one's **for** YOU. Save one for ME!

What is eaten where?

Native Americans used to eat various insects, including caterpillars, but entomophagy is no longer widely practiced in North America (or in Europe).

In **Bogota, COLOMBIA**, moviegoers happily munch on roasted atta ant abdomens instead of popcorn.

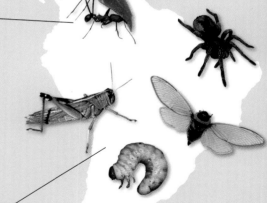

In **LATIN AMERICA** people enjoy cicadas, fire-roasted tarantulas, red-legged grasshoppers, edible ants, and beetle larvae.

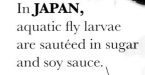

In parts of **AFRICA,** termites are eaten with cornmeal porridge, adding valuable protein.

In **CHINA,** silkworm pupae (after the silk has been removed) are considered a delicacy.

In **JAPAN,** aquatic fly larvae are sautéed in sugar and soy sauce.

In **GHANA,** winged termites are fried, roasted, or crushed and made into bread.

In **NEW GUINEA** and **AUSTRALIA**, grubs have long been traditional "bush tucker." Another favorite bush food is live ants.

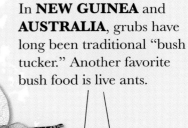

Some outdoor markets in **THAILAND** sell fried insects by the bag.

In **SOUTH AFRICA,** a huge industry has built up around the mopane worm, a large edible caterpillar (it reaches about 4 in (10 cm) in length).

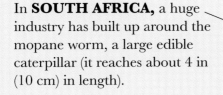

In **BALI,** you may find a dish consisting of dragonflies boiled in coconut milk and flavored with ginger and garlic.

Why? PEOPLE EAT INSECTS AND SPIDERS because they like the taste. (Some people compare the taste of fried insects to that of crispy bacon.) They are also a good source of vitamins and minerals. And they are everywhere!

Up to 80%

of the world's population **eat insects** as part of their everyday

diet.

Cricket lollipops

It's thought that some 12,000 insect species are regularly eaten by human beings. They are usually cooked.

It's nutritious! It's crunchy!

Insects are tasty, and they are nutritious—though you have to know which ones are good to eat and which ones are poisonous. However, the exoskeletons can be a little crunchy, so they take some getting used to!

Left to right: Grasshopper kebabs, cheese-flavored mealworm chips, and barbecued pupae.

Live mealworms

There are lots of good reasons for eating insects. They taste good. They are also good for you. Some are poisonous (so don't pick up any old insect and pop it in your mouth!), but choose the right cricket for a snack packed with calcium, or pick a termite for an iron boost. Here in Thailand, we sell fried insects by the bag. Get a carry-out meal and dig in!

Crispy mealworm stir-fry

Serves 2
Ingredients:
2 handfuls of mealworms
1 onion (diced)
1 red chilli (medium strength/finely sliced)
1 tablespoon sesame oil
Dash of tamari

Caution: Before you begin, read the chef's tip on the opposite page.

Method

Heat a little oil in a hot wok. Add the onion, a finely sliced chilli, and a splash of sesame oil and tamari. After one minute add the mealworm grubs. Fry for a further two minutes, then serve with chinese greens and boiled rice.

Mealworms are a good source of protein. More importantly, they are incredibly tasty.

Bee grubs in coconut cream *(Mang Non Won), Thailand*

Serves 2
Ingredients:
2 handfuls of edible grubs
1 small onion (sliced)
2 citrus leaves
10 fl oz (300 ml) coconut cream
Rice

Edible grubs

Sliced onions

Citrus leaves

Coconut cream

Rice

Mix the coconut cream, onion, and citrus leaves. Season to taste. Pour this over the bee grubs, cover, and leave in the fridge for 3-4 hours to marinate.

Wrap in pieces of linen, secure with string, and steam.

Rinse and cook the rice in boiling water for 10 minutes, then serve with the bee grubs. Enjoy your meal!

Chef's tip
Always prepare larvae by leaving in a container in the freezer for 48 hours. Then rinse under cold running water before cooking.

Edible fungus (*Cordyceps sinensis*)

A tasty snack
These dried morsels started life as wriggling caterpillars, but they were killed by a fungus that took over their bodies. They have been eaten in China for more than 2,000 years.

NOW YOU see ME...

... AND NOW YOU DON'T!
INSECTS ARE MASTERS
OF DISGUISE. AFTER ALL,
THEY DON'T WANT TO BE
EATEN. TAKE A LOOK AT
JUST HOW GOOD THEY ARE.

40

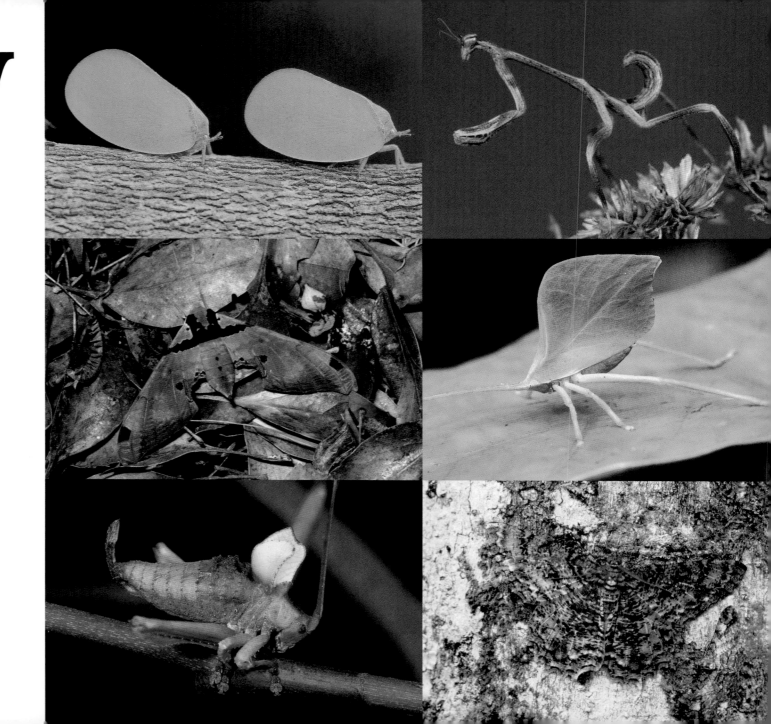

TOP ROW: leaf bug, mantis, looper moth, stick insect, spiny bugs

MIDDLE ROW: hawkmoth, katydid, katydid, leaf insect

BOTTOM ROW: katydid, geometrid moths, orchid mantis, thorn bugs, stick insect

TIME TO PLAY: TOP TRUMPS Bugs

Dragonfly

Southern hawker
(*Aeshna cyanea*)

Dragonflies are the world's fastest flying insects. They hunt on the wing, using speed and agility to capture other flying insects, such as bees and mosquitos.

NUMBER OF SPECIES	2,900
TOP SIZE	6 IN (15 CM) WIDE
TOP SPEED	36 MPH (58 KM/H)
MAX OFFSPRING	100
MAX EYE FACETS	60,000
KILLER RATING	7

Tarantula

Red-kneed tarantula
(*Brachypelma smithi*)

The giants of the spider world, tarantulas grow as big as dinner plates and can kill birds and mice with their huge fangs. Their venom is not deadly to humans.

NUMBER OF SPECIES	850
TOP SIZE	12 IN (30 CM) WIDE
TOP SPEED	4 MPH (6 KM/H)
MAX OFFSPRING	6,000
MAX EYE FACETS	8
KILLER RATING	9

Butterfly

Queen Alexandra's birdwing
(*Ornithoptera alexandrae*)

Butterflies rely on camouflage, fake eyes, or plant poisons to defend themselves. Their sensitive eyes see more colors than the eyes of any other animal.

NUMBER OF SPECIES	17,500
TOP SIZE	10 IN (28 CM) WIDE
TOP SPEED	16 MPH (25 KM/H)
MAX OFFSPRING	500
MAX EYE FACETS	4,000
KILLER RATING	2

Millipede

Armored millipede (*Polydesmus*)

Millipedes are slow-moving plant eaters. For defense they roll into a ball and rely on tough body armor. Some species also secrete potent toxins like cyanide.

NUMBER OF SPECIES	10,000
TOP SIZE	10 IN (26 CM) LONG
TOP SPEED	1.2 MPH (2 KM/H)
MAX OFFSPRING	500
MAX EYE FACETS	200
KILLER RATING	3

Beetle

Frog beetle
(*Sagra*)

About 1 in 3 insects is a beetle, making the beetles the most successful of all arthropods. Defensive weapons range from bolt-cutter jaws to boiling cyanide spray.

NUMBER OF SPECIES	370,000
TOP SIZE	6 IN (16 CM) LONG
TOP SPEED	12 MPH (20 KM/H)
MAX OFFSPRING	3,000
MAX EYE FACETS	25,000
KILLER RATING	4

Fly

Tsetse fly (*Glossina morsitans*)

Distinguished by having only 2 wings (most insects have 4), flies are aerial acrobats. They eat liquid foods, such as blood, and can spread killer diseases.

NUMBER OF SPECIES	122,000
TOP SIZE	3 IN (8 CM) LONG
TOP SPEED	25 MPH (40 KM/H)
MAX OFFSPRING	3,000
MAX EYE FACETS	4,000
KILLER RATING	7

Mantis

Praying mantis (*Mantis religiosa*)

Mantises are ambush predators. They lie in wait until prey is close, then snatch the victim with flick-action claws and bite its head off. A mantis has an ear in the middle of its chest.

NUMBER OF SPECIES	2,000
TOP SIZE	7 IN (17 CM) LONG
TOP SPEED	9 MPH (15 KM/H)
MAX OFFSPRING	1,800
MAX EYE FACETS	20,000
KILLER RATING	6

Scorpion

Imperial scorpion
(*Pandius imperator*)

Scorpions use their claws to attack and the stinging tails for defense or to paralyze prey. The potent venom of some species can paralyze a person's heart.

NUMBER OF SPECIES	1,400
TOP SIZE	7 IN (17 CM) LONG
TOP SPEED	6 MPH (10 KM/H)
MAX OFFSPRING	1,500
MAX EYE FACETS	2
KILLER RATING	10

Wasp

German wasp
(*Vespula germanica*)

Wasps prey on other insects, using their stingers to paralyze victims or lay eggs inside them. Unlike honey bees, wasps can sting repeatedly and survive.

NUMBER OF SPECIES	160,000
TOP SIZE	3 IN (7 CM) LONG
TOP SPEED	19 MPH (30 KM/H)
MAX OFFSPRING	100,000
MAX EYE FACETS	10,000
KILLER RATING	9

Bee

Bumblebee
(*Bombus terrestris*)

Bees are usually less aggressive than wasps. However, some types of honey bee carry out mass attacks that can kill a person. Honey bees die after stinging.

NUMBER OF SPECIES	20,000
TOP SIZE	2 IN (5 CM) LONG
TOP SPEED	16 MPH (25 KM/H)
MAX OFFSPRING	3,000,000
MAX EYE FACETS	20,000
KILLER RATING	9

Bug

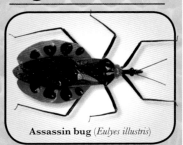

Assassin bug (*Eulyes illustris*)

Bugs use stabbing mouthparts to suck sap from plants or blood from animals. Assassin bugs prey on other insects, killing them with paralyzing venom.

NUMBER OF SPECIES	82,000
TOP SIZE	4 IN (10 CM) LONG
TOP SPEED	9 MPH (15 KM/H)
MAX OFFSPRING	1,000
MAX EYE FACETS	1,406
KILLER RATING	6

Ant

Wood ant (*Formica*)

Ants form tight-knit societies with thousands of members. The deadliest types are army and driver ants, whose marching columns kill any animal in their path.

NUMBER OF SPECIES	9,000
TOP SIZE	3 IN (7 CM) LONG
TOP SPEED	9 MPH (15 KM/H)
MAX OFFSPRING	3,500,000
MAX EYE FACETS	2,000
KILLER RATING	8

Jumping spider

Salticus spider (*Salticus*)

Jumping spiders hunt like cats. Using their superb vision, they stalk prey until close enough to pounce for the kill. They can leap 30 times their own body length.

NUMBER OF SPECIES	5,000
TOP SIZE	½ IN (16 MM) WIDE
TOP SPEED	6 MPH (10 KM/H)
MAX OFFSPRING	700
MAX EYE FACETS	8
KILLER RATING	6

Cricket

Cave cricket (*Pholeogryllus geertsi*)

Crickets have longer antennae than grasshoppers and chirp by scraping wings together (rather than by rubbing a leg). The warmer it is, the faster they chirp.

NUMBER OF SPECIES	4,000
TOP SIZE	8 IN (20 CM) LONG
TOP SPEED	6 MPH (10 KM/H)
MAX OFFSPRING	3,000
MAX EYE FACETS	2,000
KILLER RATING	2

Grasshopper

Desert locust (*Schistocerca gregaria*)

Most grasshoppers are harmless plant eaters, but some are poisonous and sport bright warning colors. Desert locusts form huge swarms that destroy crops.

NUMBER OF SPECIES	8,500
TOP SIZE	4 IN (10 CM) LONG
TOP SPEED	12 MPH (20 KM/H)
MAX OFFSPRING	2,000
MAX EYE FACETS	4,000
KILLER RATING	3

Cockroach

American cockroach (*Periplaneta americana*)

Cockroaches are among the toughest animals on Earth. They can go without food for a month, hold their breath for 45 minutes, and can survive for a week without a head.

NUMBER OF SPECIES	4,000
TOP SIZE	4 IN (10 CM) LONG
TOP SPEED	9 MPH (15 KM/H)
MAX OFFSPRING	3,000
MAX EYE FACETS	4,000
KILLER RATING	4

Woodlouse

Pill woodlouse (*Armadillidium vulgare*)

Woodlice are not insects but crustaceans that have adapted to life on land. They live in damp places and eat rotting plants. Sea-dwelling relatives can be as big as rabbits.

NUMBER OF SPECIES	4,000
TOP SIZE	1 IN (3 CM) LONG
TOP SPEED	0.6 MPH (1 KM/H)
MAX OFFSPRING	1,000
MAX EYE FACETS	80
KILLER RATING	3

Damselfly

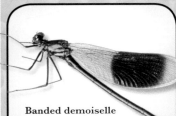

Banded demoiselle (*Calopteryx splendens*)

Damselflies are similar to dragonflies but are slimmer and rest with their wings folded rather than outstretched. They spend their early lives entirely underwater.

NUMBER OF SPECIES	2,000
TOP SIZE	7 IN (17 CM) WIDE
TOP SPEED	19 MPH (30 KM/H)
MAX OFFSPRING	300
MAX EYE FACETS	30,000
KILLER RATING	6

Tangle-web spider

Black widow (*Latrodectus mactans*)

Members of this spider family ensnare victims in tangled webs (cobwebs). The family includes the black widow, whose venomous bite can kill a person.

NUMBER OF SPECIES	2,200
TOP SIZE	2 IN (6 CM) WIDE
TOP SPEED	2 MPH (3 KM/H)
MAX OFFSPRING	3,000
MAX EYE FACETS	8
KILLER RATING	9

Moth

Promethea moth (*Callosamia promethea*)

Most moths are small and drab, but a few species are as large and spectacular as any butterfly. Promethea moths have eyespots on their wings to confuse attacking birds.

NUMBER OF SPECIES	150,000
TOP SIZE	12 IN (30 CM) WIDE
TOP SPEED	25 MPH (40 KM/H)
MAX OFFSPRING	500
MAX EYE FACETS	16,000
KILLER RATING	2

90%

of all animal species are **insects.**

One-third of these are

beetles

There are more species of beetles than there are species of plants.

What makes a beetle a beetle?

A beetle is an insect, which means it has six legs and three body parts. Most beetles have two pairs of wings, but one pair is not used for flying—they are hard cases that protect the flying wings. There are more than 300,000 species of beetle.

A person who studies beetles is called a coleopterist.

Beetles live everywhere on Earth, except in the oceans and around the freezing polar regions.

How did **this** beetle change the landscape of **AUSTRALIA?**

Rollers, tunnelers, and dwellers
There are more than 5,000 types of dung beetle. Rollers—the most advanced—roll balls of dung to a new location, using it for food or for burying their eggs in before hatching. Tunnelers bury dung and live in tunnels underneath their supply. Dwellers simply live in manure wherever they find it.

Knee deep in dirt...
That's where we'd be without dung beetles. They collect dung from the Earth's surface, and by recycling it return valuable nutrients to the soil. They keep the fly population down (and fly-borne diseases at bay) by removing dung before flies can breed. And they make the soil more moist by creating holes that enable it to absorb more rainwater.

The sacred scarab
Ancient Egyptians regarded the scarab (another name for the dung beetle) as holy. They likened the scarab to the god Khepri, who rolled the morning Sun out across the Earth every day just as a dung beetle rolls a ball of dung across the ground.

Beetle body
Armor covers much of a dung beetle's body. Concealed within it are wings, only visible when the beetle is in flight. Six legs shovel, grip, and sometimes roll dung into balls. In old dung beetles the front legs are often missing or damaged.

Dung

Cow

When the *first* people from **Europe** arrived in Australia they found many animals that were different from their own. There were no **COWS** at all, so they *slowly* INTRODUCED THEM and within no time cattle were being farmed in every state. **Cow pies** are loose and watery compared to the small pellets of kangaroos and other big animals, and the native dung beetles in Australia couldn't cope with them and left them alone. In 1966, it was clear that if something wasn't done, **Australia** would be covered in cow pies with no one to CLEAR THEM AWAY. So it was suggested that a few species of **dung beetle** should be brought from different parts of the world. By the 1980s a few species had become *established* and were *successfully* clearing away cow pies all over the country. The tiny dung beetle saved the day!

Kangaroo

Dung beetles

How did this insect **change** the **politics** of Europe**?**

Life-size cochineal insect

What is cochineal?

The cochineal insect (*Dactylopius coccus*) is a tiny scale insect that lives in tropical and subtropical South America and Mexico. It lives on cacti.

The insect produces an acid to stop other insects from eating it. The acid can be taken out of the insect's body and eggs to make a red dye.

These days cochineal is used as a food coloring. Its popularity has increased as health concerns over artificial food colorings have risen.

Anyone who is anyone must be seen in red.

Capturing the perfect red

Red is one of the most loved of all colors, and it has been for thousands of years. Throughout the world, in different cultures, red has been used to represent danger, courage, passion, violence, and beauty. However, humans would see a range of vibrant reds in nature—in flowers, on insects, the color of blood and fire—but re-creating it was another matter. European artists and dyers struggled for centuries to find a way to produce the perfect red, and until the 16th century the best reds were made from another insect, called kermes. Neolithic cave paintings in France, the Dead Sea Scrolls, and the wrappings of Egyptian mummies were all tinted with this dye. Compared to the reds in nature, however, kermes tints look dull and faded.

By the 14th century, the Incas and Aztecs in Mexico were producing an extraordinary red dye from the tiny cochineal insect. They valued the dye as much as gold. In the 1520s, Spanish invaders (conquistadors) found the Aztecs selling a beautiful red dye in their markets. They quickly learned of its secrets and shipped it back to Europe, where it produced the strongest red the world had ever seen. The dye was an instant success. Red became the color of royalty and aristocracy and Spain made a fortune selling cochineal around the world.

The Spanish kept the insect a heavily guarded secret. Most Europeans thought the dye was extracted from berries or cereals, because the dried insects looked like grains of wheat. Access to cochineal farms was tightly controlled and many unfortunate dye workers were put to death to ensure the secret was kept. Eventually, a French naturalist succeeded in smuggling out live cactus pads covered with the insects. Cochineal "ranches" were started in dozens of countries and remained the main source of red dye until synthetic dyes were produced at the end of the 1800s.

GLO-IN-THE-DARK

The twinkling lights that flit magically through woodlands on midsummer nights are **FIREFLIES (2).** They are not really flies but flying beetles, and their flashes are coded signals to mates. There are hundreds of firefly species, each with its own secret code of flashes. Some predatory fireflies even use trick codes to lure other species to their death. The glow comes from within a firefly's abdomen, where a chemical reaction releases light with near-perfect efficiency. A lightbulb wastes 90% of its energy as heat, but a firefly stays cold and releases almost 100% of the energy as light. **GLOWWORMS (1)** are the larvae of fireflies or the wingless females. The larvae can also produce light, not to attract mates but to warn predators that they taste nasty.

IT TAKES
70,000
FIREFLIES TO
MAKE AS MUCH
LIGHT AS ONE
LIGHTBULB

What other animals glow?

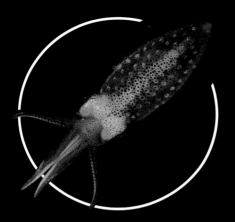

Besides fireflies, there are glowing gnats, glowing springtails, and many glowing sea animals. About 90% of deep-sea creatures produce light for one reason or another. Some, such as anglerfish, use light as a lure to catch prey. Others, including this glowing squid, spew out a cloud of glowing liquid to startle an enemy before making a quick getaway.

Do plants glow in the dark?

Organisms that produce light are described as "bioluminescent." There are no bioluminescent plants, but some mushrooms produce light, perhaps to attract tiny gnats that help spread the mushrooms' spores. The eerie glow from these mushrooms is called "foxfire" and was used for portable lighting in the world's first submarines.

How do scorpions glow?

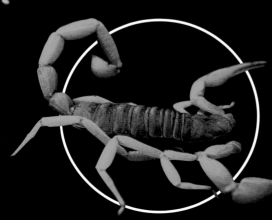

Scorpions can't produce light, but they do glow with a striking blue-green light when lit up with an ultraviolet lamp (a blacklight). The glow comes from fluorescent minerals in the skin, and nobody knows if it has a purpose. One advantage is that scorpions are very easy to find at night if you have a UV lamp!

Where does the light come from?

Fireflies, squids, and mushrooms all make light in a similar way: by making a substance called luciferin react with oxygen. Scientists have found the genes that control this chemical reaction and have figured out how to insert the genes into cancer cells so they glow. The research could lead to important new discoveries about the way cancer spreads.

Growing *up*

The way insects grow up is nothing like the way humans do. Most insects go through a dramatic transformation as they turn into adults. Often, the change is so great that the adult looks totally different from the young insect. The changing process is called *metamorphosis*.

I'm a dragonfly nymph about to change into an adult. First I climb out of my pond and up a reed, where I cling on tightly...

I split my skin for the final time and start to wriggle out.

My new skin has already formed, but at first it is very soft so I can squeeze out of the old skin. The new skin will harden after an hour or so.

Complete metamorphosis

Swallowtail butterfly

Larva (caterpillar)
Pupa (chrysalis)
Adult (butterfly)

In about 90% of insects, the young form is called a larva and looks nothing like the adult. It has no wings, no antennae, and no compound eyes. Caterpillars are the larvae of butterflies. A larva's job is simply to eat and grow. Then it forms a resting stage called a pupa. Inside the pupa, its body is broken down and rebuilt as an adult.

Simple growth

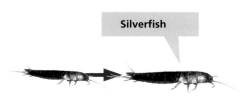

Silverfish

In a few insect species, metamorphosis doesn't happen. The youngsters are miniature replicas of the adult. They simply grow bigger, shedding their skin a few times to give room for growth.

Incomplete metamorphosis

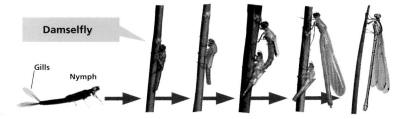

Damselfly

Gills
Nymph

Damselflies, cockroaches, and various other insects grow up in stages. The youngsters, or nymphs, look like adults but have no wings. With each molt they get more like an adult, acquiring wings at the last stage. Dragonflies and damselflies live underwater as nymphs and change the most on their final molt.

7 8 9 10 11 12

1 HR 15 MINS

How long does it take?

My wings are shrivelled for now but will slowly expand. Then I'll fly for the first time.

Just over an hour after leaving the water, I fly away to begin my adult life.

Who's the daddy?

All the arthropods on the blue page are adults. On the white page are their younger forms (larvae), before metamorphosis. See if you can match the adults to the babies. Write down the numbers and letters you think go together, then check the answers on the next page.

1

2

3

4

5

6

7

8

9

10

11

12

Match the parent to the child

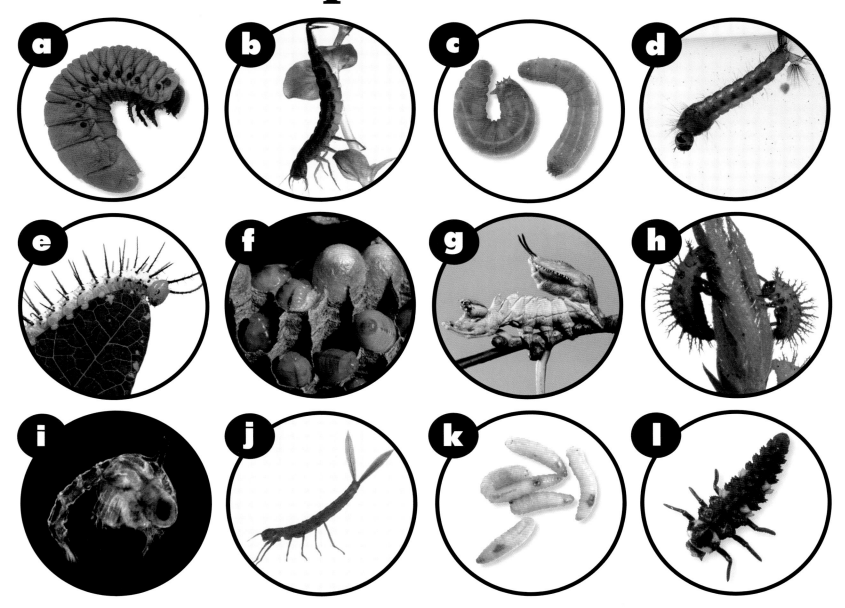

57

OUCH!
You're stepping on my wing!

Different groups (broods) of cicada emerge nearly every year somewhere in North America, but the biggest and most spectacular is called "brood ten." It is next due in late spring 2021.

Yawn...

DAY 1

I'm a young cicada—a "nymph." I live underground and feed on the root of a plant. I spend 17 years here, in the dark, without moving. It's kind of boring…

GET OUT OF MY WAY!

DAY 5

There are millions of us in the forest now. Predators will catch a lot of us, but there are far too many for the predators to eat. Most of us will survive.

ONCE IN A BLUE MOON

DATE FOR THE CALENDAR

2021
MAY 20 (ish)

The amazing periodical cicada spends precisely 13 or 17 years of its life hidden underground as a youngster. Then it crawls out in the dead of night to grow up and lead its short adult life. Every 13 or 17 years, vast numbers of cicadas emerge at once in the forests of North America. They cover the trees and fill the air with sound, creating one of the wonders of the natural world.

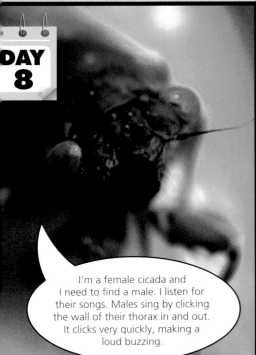

Butterfly

Orange sulfur
(*Colias eurytheme*)

Small copper
(*Lycaena phlaeas*)

Common blue
(*Polyommatus icarus*)

Small postman
(*Heliconius erato*)

Small white
(*Pieris rapae*)

Cairns birdwing
(*Ornithoptera primus*)

Queen Alexandra's
birdwing
(*Ornithotera priamus*)

Tiger
swallowtail
(*Papilio
glaucus*)

Camberwell beauty
(*Nymphalis antiopa*)

Blue morpho
(*Morpho menelaus*)

Sulfur butterfly
(*Anthocharis cardamines*)

Monarch
butterfly
(*Danaus
plexippus*)

Day flight
Most butterflies fly during the day, but some fly at dusk. None fly at night. The sun warms their flight muscles.

Antennae
Most butterflies have thin antennae. All have a small, rounded club at the tip.

Body
Butterflies tend to have smooth, thin bodies.

Feeding
Butterflies use a proboscis (which is sort of like a coiled drinking straw) to feed on nectar.

At rest
Most butterflies rest with their wings upright and together.

Pupa
A butterfly pupa, also called a chrysalis, has a protective hard shell and often hangs from a leaf.

Both butterflies and moths belong to the same group of insects: the *Lepidoptera*,

or Moth?

Butterflies evolved from moths, and they share many features. But here are some signs to help you spot the difference...

Fly by night
Most moths are active at night, though there are many that fly in daylight. They vibrate their flight muscles to warm them up.

Antennae
Many moths have feathery, brushlike antennae, which help them to sense their way at night by smell.

Body
Moths tend to be rounder than butterflies, with fuzzy bodies. The fuzz helps to keep them warm at night.

Feeding
It is hard for moths to find food at night. Many adult moths have no mouthparts and do not feed at all.

At rest
Moths usually rest with their wings open and flat, or angled slightly downward.

Pupa
Moths pupate inside a silk cocoon, which is usually on or under the ground. (However, not all moths form a cocoon.)

Female ghost moth
(*Hepialus humuli*)

Garden tiger moth
(*Arctia caja*)

Male ghost moth
(*Hepialus humuli*)

Verdant sphinx hawk moth
(*Euchloron megaera*)

Owl moth
(*Brahmaea wallichii*)

Promethea moth
(*Callosamia prometheae*)

Large emerald moth
(*Geometra papilionaria*)

Sable moth
(*Rheumaptra hastata*)

Australian regent skipper
(*Euschemon rafflesia*)

Snout moth
(*Vitessa suradeva*)

European goat moth
(*Cossus cossus*)

Puss moth
(*Cerura vinula*)

Six-spot burnet moth
(*Zygaena filipendulae*)

which means "wings of scale." They both have wings covered in tiny scales.

MEET THE FLOCKERS

The **extraordinary** story of the monarch butterfly

For such a small creature, the colorful monarch butterfly undergoes a remarkable journey. As the first fall leaves start to fall, thousands of these butterflies gather in southern *Canada* and other parts of *North America* to migrate south. Some will travel almost 2,000 miles (3,000 km), heading for the warmer climates of *California*, *Mexico*, and *Cuba*.

Caterpillar

Chrysalis

Butterfly emerging

Life **patterns**

ONE OF SEVERAL FLIGHT PATHS OF THE MONARCH BUTTERFLY IN NORTH AMERICA

1 MARCH–APRIL: The first generation of monarchs is born. They undergo full metamorphosis, from egg to caterpillar to chrysalis to adult butterfly. They mate, lay eggs, and then die.

2 MAY–JUNE: The second generation is born. Their lives follow the pattern of the first generation.

3 JULY–AUGUST: The third generation is born, undergoes metamorphosis, and dies.

4 SEPTEMBER–NOVEMBER: The fourth generation does not die so soon. They MIGRATE south on an incredibly long journey and then hibernate in a winter roost for five to seven months in Mexico or southern California. They awaken and begin mating in February and March of the NEXT SPRING, and then start the long journey north, and lay their eggs. They finally die. Young monarchs find their way back to the breeding grounds of the first generation on instinct; older butterflies don't show them the way!

At one sanctuary in Mexico, near Angangueo, it is estimated that every winter some 100 million monarch butterflies arrive from Canada and North America. The air is filled with the sound of their fluttering wings.

Monarchs are poisonous and they taste awful. Predators soon learn to avoid them.

It takes **four** generations of butterflies to make this *incredible* journey. The *fourth* generation does MOST of the work.

A Silkworm's Story

The first thing you need to know is that I am not a worm. I am the caterpillar of a Chinese moth, and the single thread I spin for my cocoon has been harvested by people to use as silk for at least 4,000 years.

Jaws

Antenna

Eyes

Spinneret

My species no longer lives in the wild. In fact, we are entirely dependent on human beings for reproduction. I'm a male, and my feathery antennae help me to pick up the scent of a female.

The thread is spun from a small tube just beneath my mouth.

Females cannot fly, while males cannot fly very well. So a male needs a female to be close by, or he will not find her. The adult males die soon after mating. The females die after laying eggs.

The cocoons have to be sorted. The finer ones will be used for silk cloth. Some are rejected due to imperfections such as staining or holes.

Why was this **caterpillar** worth **more** than GOLD to the people of ancient **China?**

Silkworms—the caterpillars of silk moths—feed on mulberry leaves. There are several varieties of mulberry tree, but the silkworm eats only one: the Chinese white mulberry. Surprisingly, leaves of the mulberry can vary enormously in size and shape, even those on the same branch.

Life-size three-day-old silkworm caterpillar (*Bombyx mori*)

It's because of the secret that surrounded silk, the continuous thread that is spun by the silkworm when making its cocoon.

It's the wrong tree!
All around the world, people were eager to discover the secret of silk. In fact, mulberry trees were introduced to England in the 1600s, when King James I instructed all who were able to plant mulberry trees to develop a silk industry. However, the wrong type of tree was planted.

 # The empress, her drink, the moth, and her larva

The story goes (according to Chinese legend) that a Chinese empress was sitting under a mulberry tree, enjoying a hot drink, when a silkworm cocoon fell into her cup. The empress was surprised to see the **cocoon** unraveling. She began to experiment with silkworms and developed the use of silk in weaving cloth around 2,400 BCE.

The making of silk was to become one of the most closely guarded **secrets** of all time, as it was so important to the Chinese economy (for thousands of years, it was more **precious** than **gold**). Outside China, people had no idea an animal was involved. Writing in

70 BCE, the famous Roman historian Pliny stated: "Silk was obtained by removing the down from the leaves with the help of water…".

At first, only the emperor wore silk, but gradually its use spread among the Chinese. Eventually, it was used for things such as bowstrings on musical instruments and for fishing lines.

The humble silkworm even lent its name to an ancient trading network, the **Silk Route**. This route ran from China through the deserts of Central Asia to the West (the route was only given this name in the 1800s). All kinds of things were traded, but for a long time silk was the most valuable.

Old Chinese proverb

With time and patience the mulberry leaf becomes a silk gown. Patience is power;

WHOO-whoo

SPOT the FAKE

A **cunning way** to defend yourself from attack is to pretend to be something nasty. All the creatures on the top row here are mimicking the dangerous animals below. The disguises aren't perfect, but they are good enough to fool a predator for the few seconds it takes to make a getaway.

The caterpillar of a Costa Rican hawkmoth can inflate its body to imitate the head of a venomous viper. Glaring eyespots complete the disguise.

Viceroy (top) and monarch (bottom) butterflies mimic each other. Both species are foul tasting to birds, and the similar patterns reinforce the message.

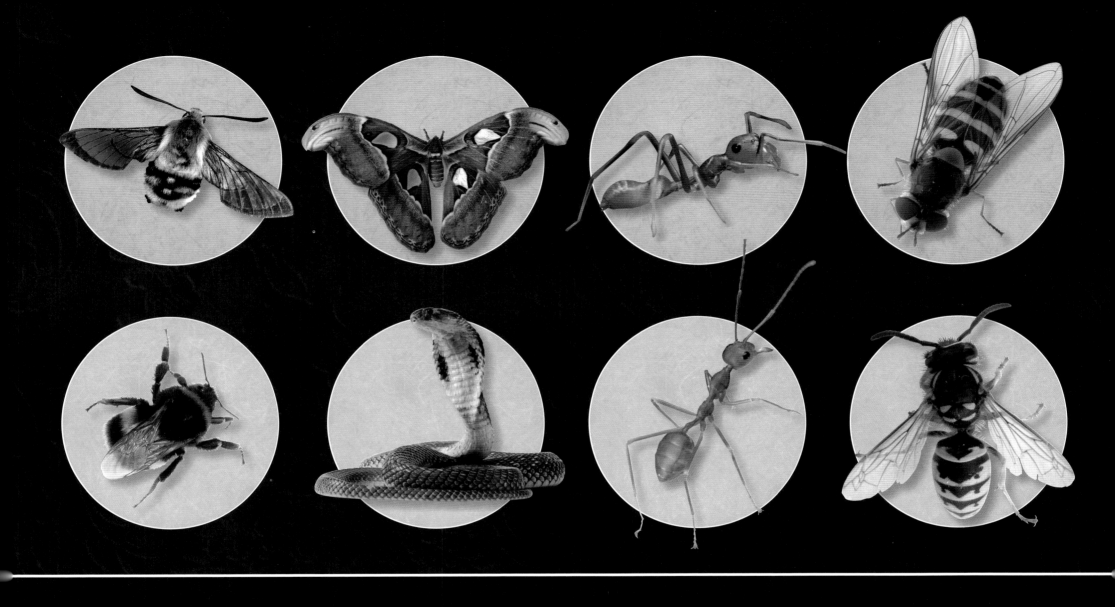

Bushy antennae and outspread wings are clues that the top "bee" here is really just a harmless moth. The disguise scares off birds that have learned to avoid bees.

Look closely at the wingtips of the Atlas moth. Some people think they resemble the head of a deadly cobra poised to spit out venom.

Count the legs on the top "ant." It's actually a jumping spider disguised as an ant so it can lurk near the ants' colony for protection.

The hoverfly's wasplike stripes are there to fool birds, but even humans are sometimes afraid of these harmless insects.

WHAT AM I?

THIS IS WHAT THE WORLD WOULD LOOK LIKE IF YOU WERE AS SMALL AS AN ANT. ALL THE PICTURES ARE CLOSE-UPS OF ARTHROPODS—CAN YOU GUESS WHAT THEY ARE?

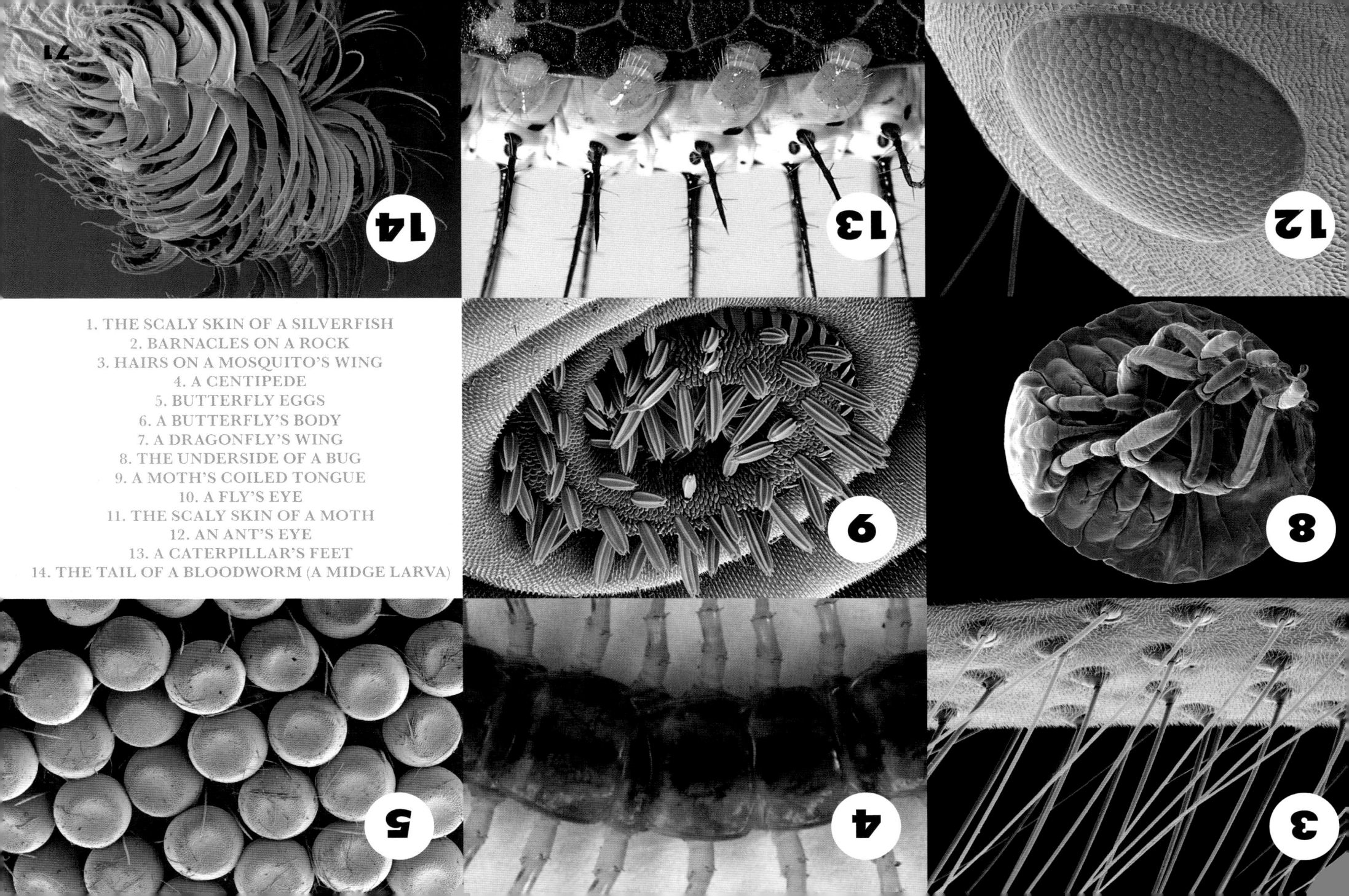

1. THE SCALY SKIN OF A SILVERFISH
2. BARNACLES ON A ROCK
3. HAIRS ON A MOSQUITO'S WING
4. A CENTIPEDE
5. BUTTERFLY EGGS
6. A BUTTERFLY'S BODY
7. A DRAGONFLY'S WING
8. THE UNDERSIDE OF A BUG
9. A MOTH'S COILED TONGUE
10. A FLY'S EYE
11. THE SCALY SKIN OF A MOTH
12. AN ANT'S EYE
13. A CATERPILLAR'S FEET
14. THE TAIL OF A BLOODWORM (A MIDGE LARVA)

WHY have *these* been kept in *specially* made **CAGES** for more **than** 2,000 YEARS ?

Cricket

... BECAUSE THEY ...
make *sweet* music

In **many** countries around the world, people keep crickets as *household pets.* **WHY?** Because they ***sing***, and it's rather a **pleasant** song to hear. *(It's also a good antiburglar device—one minute a cricket will be merrily singing away, only to stop if a visitor approaches.)* BY THE WAY, they sing by **rubbing** the edge of one wing against the edge of another—they DON'T open their mouths and **belt** out a song like us!

The cricket moves the wings together to make a sound.

The cricket makes the noise it produces louder by raising its wings. It also has a clear area on the wing (called a mirror) that helps to increase the volume.

OF COURSE, the cricket doesn't sing to entertain us! It sings to attract a mate!

TOP ten

Tadpole shrimp.
Ever wanted a prehistoric pet? The tadpole shrimp (*Triops cancriformis*) is probably the oldest species of animal alive. It's easy to keep. All you need is a plastic tank full of mineral water, some *Triops* eggs, and fish food. Keep the tank in a warm, sunny spot. The eggs will hatch and grow into 3 inch- (8 cm-) long living fossils. The only snag is that they like to eat each other...

Honey bees.
You need special equipment to look after honey bees, including protective clothing and hives. But once it's all set up, the bees do the work for you and reward you with lots of honey. In winter, when there are no flowers to feed the bees, you'll have to feed them yourself.

Atlas moth.
The world's biggest moth (in wing area) reaches 10 in (25 cm) wide. Buy eggs online and watch the bizarre caterpillars grow enormous before they spin their silk cocoons. They eat many types of leaf, making them easy to rear. However, the adults can't feed and live for only two weeks.

Hermit crab.
Marine hermit crabs (*Pagurus*, below) need aquariums, but the land hermit crab (*Coenobita*) is much easier to look after. It just needs a tank with sand, a dish of water, somewhere to hide, and a range of empty shells to move into as it grows.

Ants.
To create your very own ants' nest, search for the wingless queens that leave ants' nests in summer. Put a queen in a small, escape-proof box (or ready-made ant farm) with some fine soil, damp cotton balls, and sugar water. In no time, she'll lay eggs and your colony will be on its way. Be careful which type of ant you use. The wood ants here are aggressive and squirt acid—they don't make good pets!

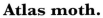
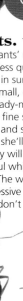

PeT Bugs!

Mombasa train millipede. Two hundred legs and they never, ever trip! The tiny feet feel like a strip of velcro when they walk on you—a very strange feeling. Trained millipedes make good pets. They are docile and calm, with few needs except a supply of fruit and a large tank with a floor of damp soil. Millipedes can secrete a defensive liquid and so need to be handled with care—never touch your mouth or eyes after holding one.

5

2

Stick insects. Sticks, leaves, logs, and bark are some of the things these amazing insects mimic. Most are easy to keep, but watch out for population explosions, since some species don't need mates to produce babies! Feeding is easy—bramble leaves are a favorite for most stick insects.

Red-kneed tarantula. Probably the best arthropod pet in the world. It's easy to keep and can live for nearly 30 years. If you buy a young, captive-bred one, you can train it to be picked up. The nearly half-inch- (1-cm-) long fangs deliver a potent venom, but they are only used for biting prey (usually). Live crickets from pet stores make ideal victims. If the tarantula loses a leg, a whole new one grows back in its place.

1

Praying mantis. Watch as the mantis slowly stalks its prey, never letting it out of its sight. Then... WHAM! The mantis strikes with lightning speed. Mantises are fascinating animals with huge eyes that follow you everywhere. They need branches to clamber on, water to drink, and a supply of live insects, such as crickets, which you can buy from pet stores.

3

Imperial scorpion. Scorpions are not for beginners—the pincers can nip and the stings can hurt. However, this species—the world's biggest scorpion—rarely attacks and its sting is not deadly. Imperial scorpions like to live in groups and are most active at night. Their babies look like white woodlice and cling to their mom's back.

4

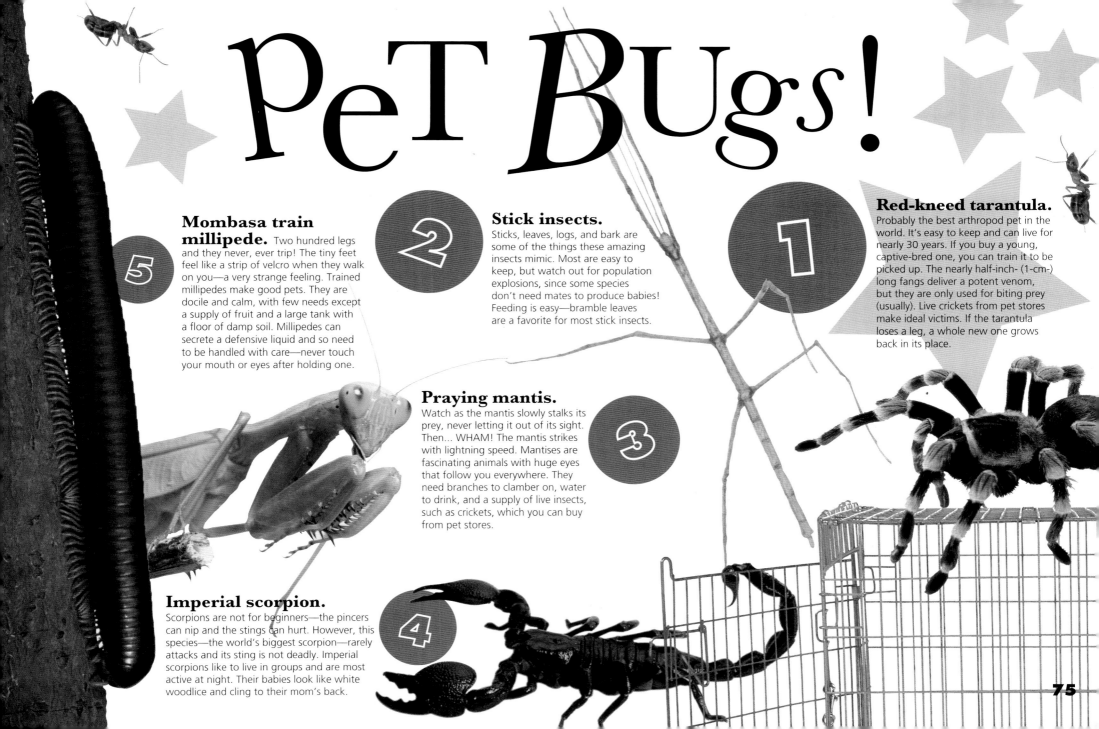

LOCUST PLAGUE

A locust *attack* can be **devastating**.

JUST FOLLOWING THE CROWD...

Desert locusts normally lead solitary lives, but they can undergo an amazing change. If enough food grows, lots of locusts are able to hatch. The overcrowding makes them totally change the way they look: they become shorter and turn a different color.

African desert locust (*Schistocerca gregaria*)

> WILL I STAY A LONELY LOCUST OR BECOME A PARTY ANIMAL?

Locusts will remain **solitary** *unless* there are lots of other locusts around. They stay green and cause relatively little damage.

Swarming locusts also change the way they act: they become "**gregarious**," forming a swarm that acts as one unit, *devastating* crops.

WANTED

FROM THE INFAMOUS LOCUST GANG—HE'S **DESTRUCTIVE!**

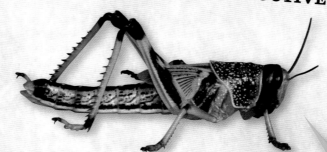

Huge REWARD

... if **you** can find a means of stopping the desert locust from wreaking **havoc**.

What's the solution? Unfortunately, once the **African desert locust** descends, there is nothing a farmer can do but watch as crops are hungrily devoured. Scientists are trying to help by predicting where a swarm may break out, but the swarms are so big, they quickly take control.

> I just need to eat. What's the problem?

A cloud appears

Locust swarms first appear as a dark cloud on the horizon. They can travel 80 miles (130 km) a day, so when they settle, they are hungry! They will strip a field in minutes, leaving it bare, and they are widespread. Swarms have been reported in at least 60 of the world's countries.

Above: Locust eating
Right: Swarm of locusts on crops

What's for lunch?

Locusts have taste and touch sensors all over their bodies. They can quickly assess whether or not a crop is good to eat.

85¢

October 10, 1996

The International paper

Plague returns

Farmers in large parts of Eastern Africa have been reporting increasing numbers of locust swarms. These insects have been feared by farmers in huge parts of Africa and Asia for thousands of years. A locust can eat its own weight in a day, and it is greedy. Just under half a square mile (1 sq km) may contain 80 million of the creatures, while a swarm can cover hundreds of miles (kilometers). During one plague in Somalia, the locusts devoured enough food to feed 400,000 people for a whole year.

A locust swarm passes over.

77

Who can you eat and who would be poisonous?

Don't dig in unless you're sure it's safe!

(Background text, repeated throughout the page:) Let's eat... a witchety grub, a silkworm pupa, a few beetles and mealworms, some moths, perhaps a butterfly, a couple of cicada pupae, a handful of grubs and maggots, a huge spider (let's try a tarantula), a caterpillar or two, a handful of honeypot ants, a grasshopper and a cricket.

Chocolate surprise!

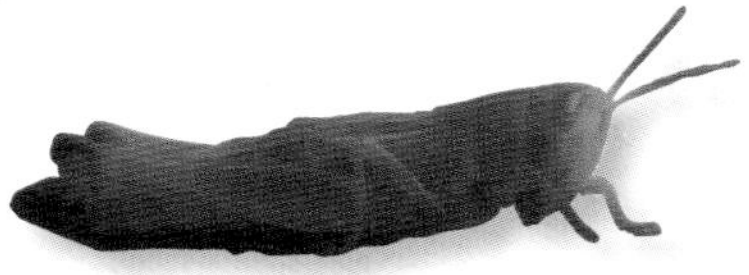

Ingredients:
Good quality chocolate
Dried edible crickets
or edible grasshoppers

NB: Insects need to be prepared carefully before being eaten—and some are poisonous.

Melt the chocolate over a bowl of hot water.

Pour the chocolate into pots until they are half-full.

Add a dried cricket or grasshopper to each pot.

Fill up the pots with chocolate and leave to set.

A tasty surprise in every one!

Who's for dinner?

Check out the menu...

THE MENU

1. One sumptuously smelly sock

2. A lovely, sweet, fleshy baby

3. A delectable dollop of dung

4. A crunchy coil of cardboard

5. Your very own mother

6. A tower of tasty tomes

7. Nothing at all, not a crumb!

All kinds of arthropods dine on live humans. The **head louse** clambers through your hair and snacks on blood by biting your skin. **Mosquitos** land for one bite and fly away full of blood. Scabies mites dig tunnels inside your skin and make you itch. Botfly maggots burrow into muscles and sit there for weeks, eating your flesh.

Fruit flies like the taste of rotting fruit—the natural source of alcohol. Just like humans, they get drunk and pass out if they have too much. But they never get addicted.

Not many animals can digest wood, but **termites** can. If they get into your house, they can eat their way through floorboards and beams until the whole building collapses.

Silverfish are fond of books, but rather than reading them they eat the glue that holds the pages together. Failing that, they eat the pages themselves. They aren't greedy—they survive on tiny amounts and can live for a year without eating anything.

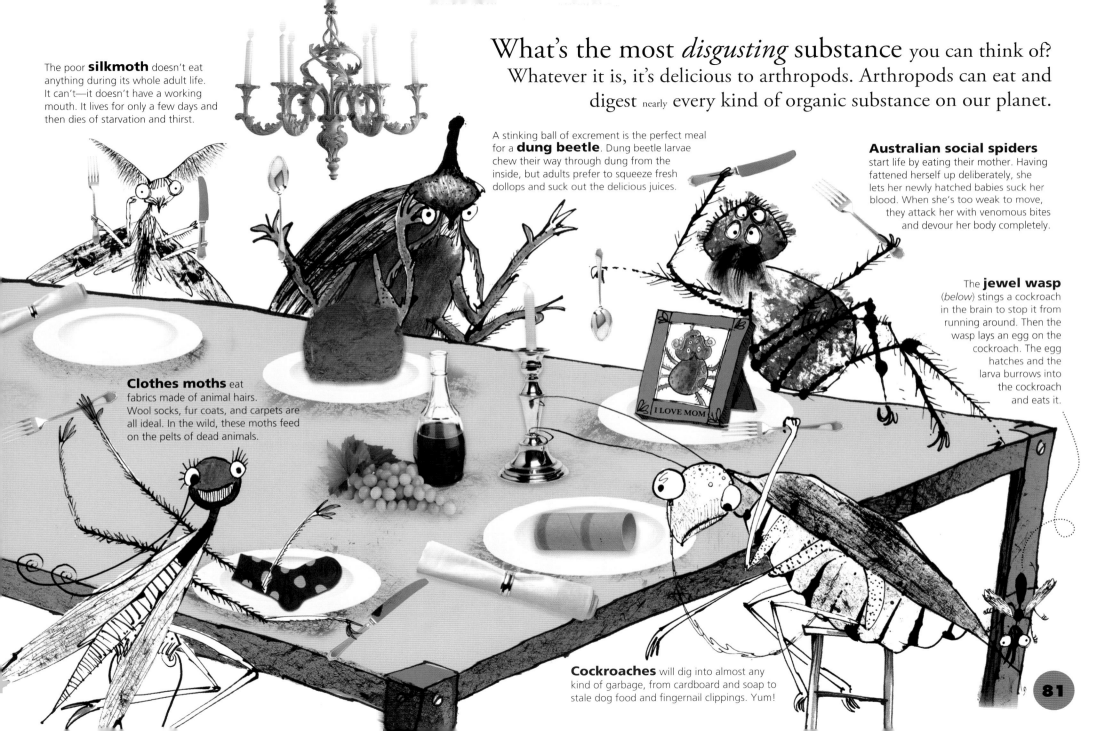

The poor **silkmoth** doesn't eat anything during its whole adult life. It can't—it doesn't have a working mouth. It lives for only a few days and then dies of starvation and thirst.

What's the most *disgusting* substance you can think of?
Whatever it is, it's delicious to arthropods. Arthropods can eat and digest nearly every kind of organic substance on our planet.

A stinking ball of excrement is the perfect meal for a **dung beetle**. Dung beetle larvae chew their way through dung from the inside, but adults prefer to squeeze fresh dollops and suck out the delicious juices.

Australian social spiders start life by eating their mother. Having fattened herself up deliberately, she lets her newly hatched babies suck her blood. When she's too weak to move, they attack her with venomous bites and devour her body completely.

The **jewel wasp** (*below*) stings a cockroach in the brain to stop it from running around. Then the wasp lays an egg on the cockroach. The egg hatches and the larva burrows into the cockroach and eats it.

Clothes moths eat fabrics made of animal hairs. Wool socks, fur coats, and carpets are all ideal. In the wild, these moths feed on the pelts of dead animals.

I LOVE MOM

Cockroaches will dig into almost any kind of garbage, from cardboard and soap to stale dog food and fingernail clippings. Yum!

Crime Scene Insects

A CRIME HAS BEEN COMMITTED
... and a BODY found in the woods.

You may be surprised to learn that insects can play an important role in the police investigation that follows. HOW? Well, their presence and stage of development tell a FORENSIC ENTOMOLOGIST all sorts of otherwise hidden information.

OLICE LINE DO NOT CROSS

POLICE LINE DO NOT CROSS

DON'T MOVE ANYTHING. I AM AN ENTOMOLOGIST AND I'M HERE TO HELP INVESTIGATE THIS CRIME.

1

ALL BODIES decompose. Insects help this process, but they do it in a particular order. First to arrive are the blowflies (the bluebottles and greenbottles) and the flesh flies.

The blowflies lay eggs, which hatch into larvae, or maggots, within 16 to 25 hours. The larvae will become pupae between 6 and 12 days later (depending on the temperature). In the heat of summer, the process can be very quick.

AN ENTOMOLOGIST CAN TELL WHEN BLOWFLY EGGS WERE LAID BY THEIR STAGE OF DEVELOPMENT.

❶ Larval stages see the larvae molt, growing each time. After a third molt, the larvae leave the decomposing body to pupate. They will wriggle off to the surrounding soil, or into the clothes.

❷ Freshly formed pupae are pale in color. They darken to a deep brown after a few hours.

❸ A few days later the adult fly emerges, leaving its empty case (the evidence of a complete cycle).

EVIDENCE TAG
Bluebottle fly

Bluebottle eggs

EVIDENCE

EVIDENCE TAG
Bluebottle maggots

EVIDENCE

THE SCIENCE PART > All bodies break down, or decompose, after death. If they didn't, we'd be swamped in them. Insects play a vital role in decomposition and they do it in a fairly predictable way.

We don't know when the murder happened.

We know how to find out...

The insects can tell us!

POLICE LINE DO NOT CROSS

POLICE LINE DO NOT CROS

Blowfly emerges from pupa

LATER: Beginning from three to six months after death, an entomologist will expect to find cheese fly larvae (notably *Piophila casei*). *P. casei* larvae are about one-third of an inch (8 mm) in length and are sometimes known as cheese skippers because they can leap up to 6 in (15 cm)! Increasing numbers of beetles will also appear, including hide beetles and ham beetles.

2

EVIDENCE TAG

Red-legged
ham
beetle

EVIDENCE

AFTER SIX MONTHS: Hide beetles will still be present, and will have been joined by skin beetles and carcass beetles. These beetles have tough, chewing mouthparts that can cope with the drying skin and flesh. Then will come moth larvae and mites, to feed on the hair.

3

Skin beetle

EVIDENCE

83

A MOUSE'S TALE

THE DIRECTOR'S CUT

Fly larvae can take months to turn a human body into a skeleton, but in warm weather they can strip small animals of flesh in under a week. Watch what happens when a field mouse dies at the height of summer...

TAKE 1

OH GOSH! I'M NOT SURE I CAN WATCH THIS!

MONDAY The odor of the dead mouse attracts blowflies. They mate, lay eggs, and leave.

THURSDAY Internal organs, muscles, and fat are quickly consumed by a writhing mass of larvae.

TUESDAY Newly hatched larvae enter the body through weak spots such as the ears, eyes, and anus.

WEDNESDAY Next they breach the rotting skin.

FRIDAY If skin and other tough tissues don't become dry and hard, the larvae eat them as well.

SATURDAY Only bones are left. The larvae wriggle away to pupate.

And I'm afraid
that's all folks!

By the way, I'm the larva (maggot) of a bluebottle fly.
I use the hooks in my mouth to grind flesh.
I'm not really this big, I've been magnified
100 times! I normally look like this...

BUZZ

START

1

2

Shhh! Take a sneaky shortcut. ↓

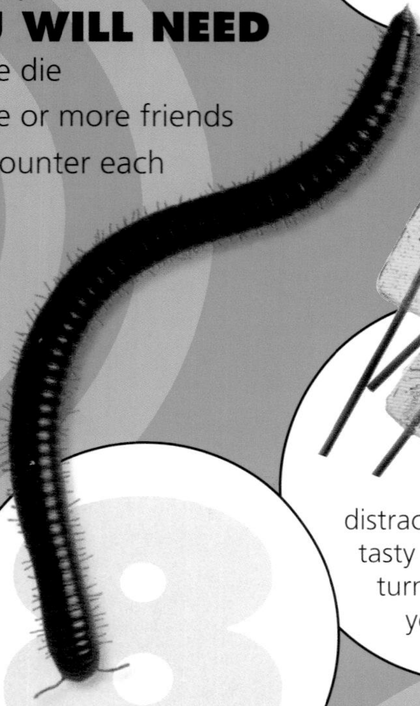

4

You get STUNG. **Ouch**. Miss a turn while you wipe away your tears.

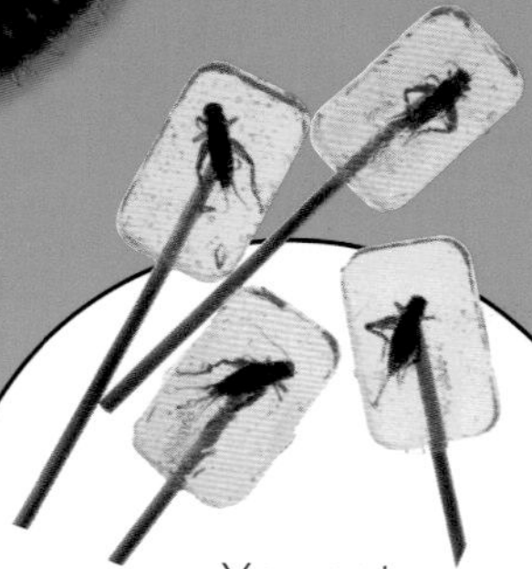

TO PLAY BUZZMANIA YOU WILL NEED
- One die
- One or more friends
- A counter each

HOW TO PLAY
Place your counters at the start and take turns rolling the die and moving your counters. Good luck!

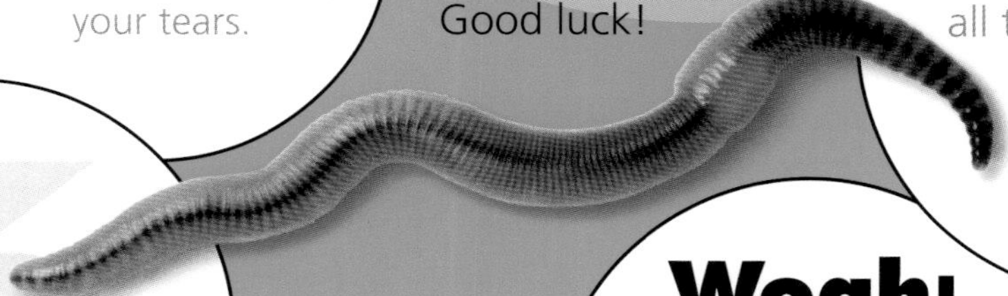

I'm not an arthropod; I'm an earthworm. Slide all the way back to my tail...

5

6

Woah!
Hitch a ride on a centipede... move forward 4 spaces.

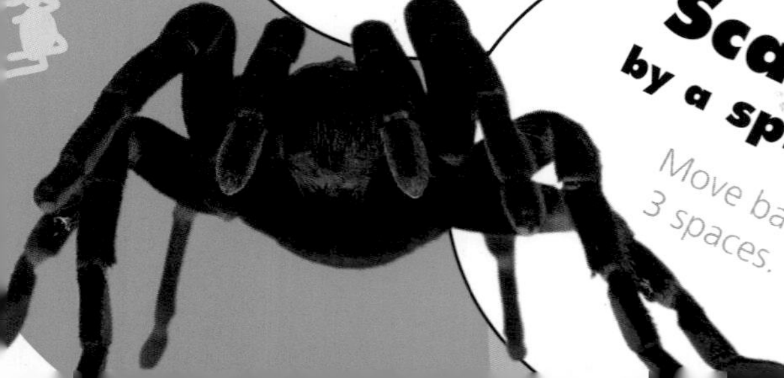

7

You get distracted by a shop of tasty morsels. Miss a turn while you fill your tummy.

Scared by a spider!
Move back 3 spaces.

8

Congratulations—you manage to get a lift on a butterfly. Move forward 5 spaces.

11

Oh no! You've been bitten by a hungry mosquito. Miss a turn while you try not to scratch that itch.

MAKE YOUR OWN BUZZ COUNTER
- Draw a bug on some cardboard
- Cut it out.
- Color it in.

MANIA

Hitch a ride on a passing locust. HOP forward 1 space.

Take another sneaky shortcut!

A firefly helps you see in the dark... ...move forward 1 space.

RUN! You get chased by a swarm of bees. Quick, move forward 4 spaces.

You're stuck in some honey. Miss a turn.

FINISH

winner!

You get stuck in a web. Miss a turn.

So near, and yet so far. You get stung by a fat-tailed scorpion and rushed to the hospital. You have a long stay, so you'd better start again.

In a hurry? Patience is a virtue. Slow down and crawl back 6 spaces.

Take a snooze and miss a turn.

Zzz

87

NOW YOU *see* me...

I AM A WALKING STICK INSECT FROM COSTA RICA.

All work and no play

Leaf-cutter ants live in enormous colonies. The colonies work because each member has a particular job to do. It's hard and they stick to it day and night. So what do they do? They are farmers.

Who is the biggest?

Winged Male
Prince!

Major
Guard

Queen
Queen!

Media
Gardener

Minima
Nurse

Maxima
Leaf cutter

Who is the smallest?

I am a **leaf cutter.** I fetch and carry leaves back to the nest. I cut them to size if necessary.

Some of us make sure the pathways to and from the nest are kept free of debris. You could call me a **roadsweeper.**

How do we know where to go to find the best leaves? We leave a scent trail.

There can be up to 10,000 of us **males** in one nest, though we only stay here part of the year. Our job is to mate, usually with queens from another nest.

So, do you want to know what happens to all those leaves? Well, millions of ants use them to create subterranean fungus gardens by licking and chewing them to a pulp. The fungus "eats" the pulp and we eat the fungus.

I am the **queen** and the workers are all my daughters. If I die, the nest dies.

Only a third of the ants   in a nest

I'm a **guard.**
I'm here in case of attack. I'll defend the leafcutter below from flies as it can't use its jaws when carrying.

I'm a **phorid fly.** If I can, I'll lay an egg on an ant's head. The hatchling maggots will find the head an easy meal!

I'm a **soldier**. Don't poke a finger into our nest or I'll slice into you with my strong jaws.

The **fungus gardens** are located underground, and they can be huge: many times the size of a football field. That's because to cultivate enough fungus, the ants must collect massive quantities of leaves, bit by tiny bit. Galleries are stacked above each other, sometimes to a depth of 20 feet (6 meters).

come out to collect leaves. The others beaver away in darkness.

ARMY ANTS

NEWS ALERT > THEY'RE COMING!

You turn at a rustle on the forest floor. Looking closely, you notice that a surprisingly large number of small insects are scrambling to escape. The rustle grows louder, now accompanied by a distinct hissing, and you begin to notice ants. Thousands of ants. These are killers, and they will overcome and eat whatever lies in their path, cutting it apart and taking it back to their nest. They can quickly subdue centipedes, scorpions, tarantulas, and even vertebrates such as lizards and geckos.

I'm a winged male driver ant. Look at my sausage-shaped abdomen.

Winged male
Ant no. 240300
Nickname:
Sausage fly

The marching column is made up of female ants, none of whom can lay eggs. They are the workers and there may be 20 million of them. There are very few males.

Large prey such as a scorpion is no obstacle to army ants. A single ant may discover it, and will then release chemicals to draw other ants toward it. The scorpion will soon be buried under a mass of ants.

92

...1,000s of **army ants.**

Army ants are social insects, working together to form colonies that are highly efficient at tasks such as rearing young and subduing prey. They move their home frequently, since otherwise they would soon run out of food. They can even build living bridges to cross obstacles on the forest floor.

So who are the killers?

There are two main types of ant that forage in armies: the army ants of North, South, and Central America, and the driver ants of Africa. There are some differences. Army ants have a powerful sting. Driver ants use sharp mandibles (jaws) to slice away at their victims. Army ants can't kill large vertebrates, but driver ants can—they may overpower a chicken, or an injured pig. Most large creatures can move out of the way, but arthropods can't move quickly enough. In Africa, driver ants have been known to raid villages, which can be helpful. The inhabitants simply move out while the ants clean out the cockroaches and mice that may have seen it as a safe home. All army ants form temporary homes, called bivouacs, constructing them by hooking themselves together.

I protect the worker ants with my powerful jaws. Above is our home, a bivouac of living ants.

93

Ants climbing a mountain

Ants have been eaten all around the world for thousands of years. This recipe is for a pretty fancy-looking dish, but some people think nothing of plucking an ant from its nest and eating it.

Some **honey pot ants** act as pantries for their nest. Their abdomens are so full of nectar, they cannot move. Apparently, they are very sweet to eat.

NUTRITION INFORMATION		
Typical Values	per 100g	per 30g SERVING
Energy Values	950kj 227kcal	285kj 68kcal
Protein	5g	1.5g
Carbohydrate	50g	15g
Fat	0.3g	0.1g
Calcium	5mg	1.5mg
Iron	0.6mg	0.2mg

NUTRITION INFORMATION		
Typical Values	per 100g	per 30g SERVING
Energy Values	150kj 36kcal	45kj 11kcal
Protein	13.9g	4.2g
Carbohydrate	2.9g	0.9g
Fat	3.5g	1.1g
Calcium	47.mg	14.3mg
Iron	5.7mg	1.7mg

Australian weaver ants are difficult to grab, since their bite is painful, but they can be eaten. They are said to have a lemony flavor.

Ingredients

Dried seaweed

Grated potato

Dried black ants

Small chili

Cooking oil

SERVES 2

Finely chop the red chili.

Heat a little oil in a frying pan and gently fry the grated potato until softened.

Add the chili to the potato. Arrange the seaweed on a plate and spoon the potato on top.

Sprinkle the ants on top of the dish, and serve.

Never eat an insect if you don't know it's **safe** to do so.

Surprisingly enough, some people are allergic to insects. They are not unlike shellfish, and some people cannot eat shellfish.

A nice *sprinkling* of *ants!*

There are at least **9,000** species of ant!

Who is in the **hive**?

Some bees are solitary, but not honeybees

Honeybees live in hives containing up to 80,000 individuals

Each of

buzzzzzzzzzzzz *ZZ* zzz

buzzzzzzzzzzzzzz *ZZ* zzz

buzzzzzzzzzzzzz *ZZ* zzz

The **Queen**

A hive has just one queen and her job is to lay eggs. Lots of eggs. In fact, she will lay up to 2,000 eggs each day! Most of these will be fertilized and develop into female worker bees. Those that are unfertilized become male bees (drones). What happens if she dies or stops laying eggs? The workers feed a larva on royal jelly, a food so rich that the chosen larva will develop into a new queen.

Queen honeybees reach between ½–¾ in (15 and 20 mm).

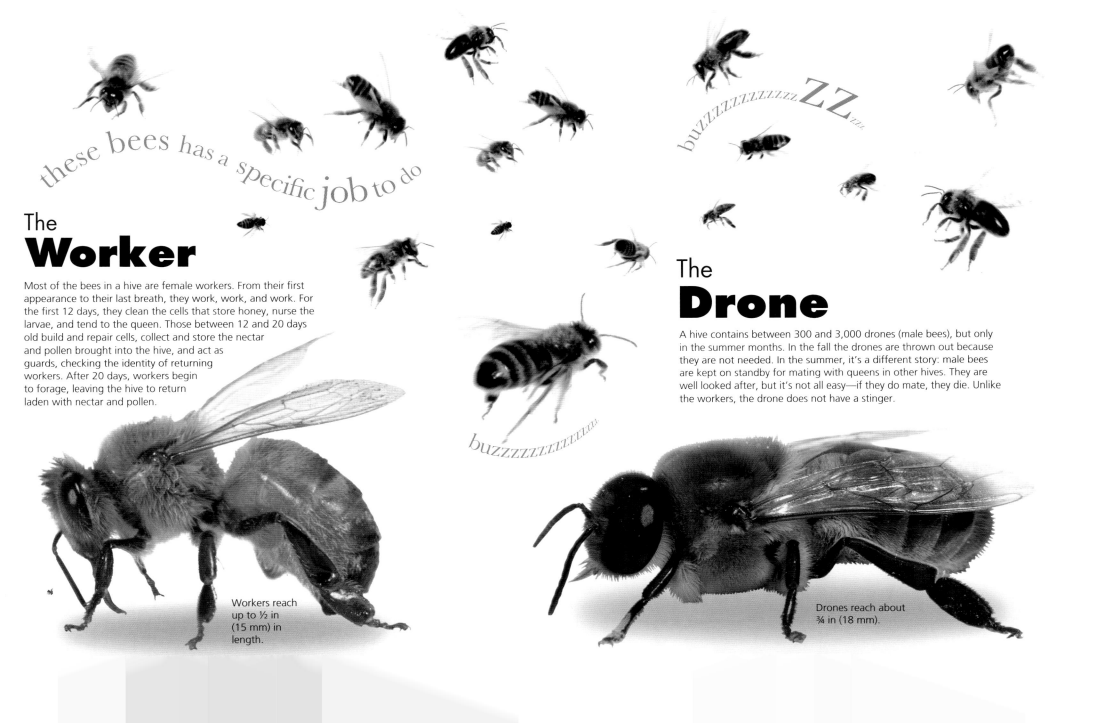

these bees has a specific job to do

buzzZZZZZZZZZZZ ZZ zzz

The
Worker

Most of the bees in a hive are female workers. From their first appearance to their last breath, they work, work, and work. For the first 12 days, they clean the cells that store honey, nurse the larvae, and tend to the queen. Those between 12 and 20 days old build and repair cells, collect and store the nectar and pollen brought into the hive, and act as guards, checking the identity of returning workers. After 20 days, workers begin to forage, leaving the hive to return laden with nectar and pollen.

buzzZZZZZZZZZZZZ

The
Drone

A hive contains between 300 and 3,000 drones (male bees), but only in the summer months. In the fall the drones are thrown out because they are not needed. In the summer, it's a different story: male bees are kept on standby for mating with queens in other hives. They are well looked after, but it's not all easy—if they do mate, they die. Unlike the workers, the drone does not have a stinger.

Workers reach up to ½ in (15 mm) in length.

Drones reach about ¾ in (18 mm).

How did **this**

There are lots of different flavored honeys. Flavor depends on the flowers the bees visited when collecting the nectar.

Beeswax crayons last longer then other crayons and the colors can be mixed. Blue and yellow *will* make green.

Beeswax is a perfect material for candle-making. Beeswax candles smell of honey—and they don't drip.

produce
this honey?

As well as so many other things that we find useful?

Honeybees are incredibly useful to us. In addition to stealing their honey, we use beeswax for an almost endless list of items, from crayons and creams to polishes and soaps. Of course, bees don't actually make the honey or wax for human use. Honey is a product of nectar, which is collected by worker bees from flowers and thickened in the hive for use as bee food. Wax is produced by young bees when they are building and repairing their hive. Each bee will produce a tiny flake of wax and some 500,000 of these go into every 1 lb (0.5 kg) of beeswax. The bees use the flakes to shape honeycomb cells into which the eggs are laid. Humans find hundreds of additional uses.

Light honey

Comb **honey**

Spun **honey**

In its lifetime each honeybee will probably only produce just 1 teaspoon of honey.

Honeybees provide us with an amazing amount of products, including honey (which we use to spread on bread and as a sweetener for baking goodies such as biscuits and cookies and bread), wax, candles, polish, varnish, crayons, as well as all sorts of lotions and potions and creams. It's amazing when you think that each honeybee will probably produce just 1 teaspoon of honey in its lifetime.

Skyscraper

How can this tiny insect build an **air-conditioned**, **multiroomed** tower with walls as hard as **concrete**?

The London landmark known as the Gherkin is built to take advantage of natural air-conditioning, drawing in air like a termite mound.

Compass termite mounds are found in northern Australia. They are always orientated a certain way.

This umbrella mound was built by African termites to withstand heavy rain.

For a start, he needs a lot of friends, and it can still take up to 50 years to complete. Yet for their size, termites build the largest structures of any living creature! Termites live in huge colonies. Their mounds are built to help them survive the hot and dry climates they inhabit and to protect them from predators. Different types of termite build mounds of different shapes and sizes.

Termite queens can grow to more than 6 in (15 cm)!

Termites are little more than ¼ inch (**1 cm**) in length, but they can build mounds that are taller than 20 ft (**6 m**).

This Australian cathedral mound may be around 100 years old.

I'm an average height, but just look at how **BIG** this tower is!

A feat of engineering

Outside, the temperature may reach 104°F (40°C), but inside, a termite mound maintains a constant, comfortable temperature. It's a perfect environment for food pantries, gardens, and, of course, nurseries for all those baby termites. Dedicated chambers for these purposes are placed at specific points inside the mound, and they usually have arched ceilings (for strength). There's even a royal chamber for the king and queen. A clever system of tunnels and chimneys ensures that air flows around the nest, and the mound even has foundations so it doesn't collapse, just like a brick-built house. And all this is achieved without teams of architects and engineers poring over plans and drawings.

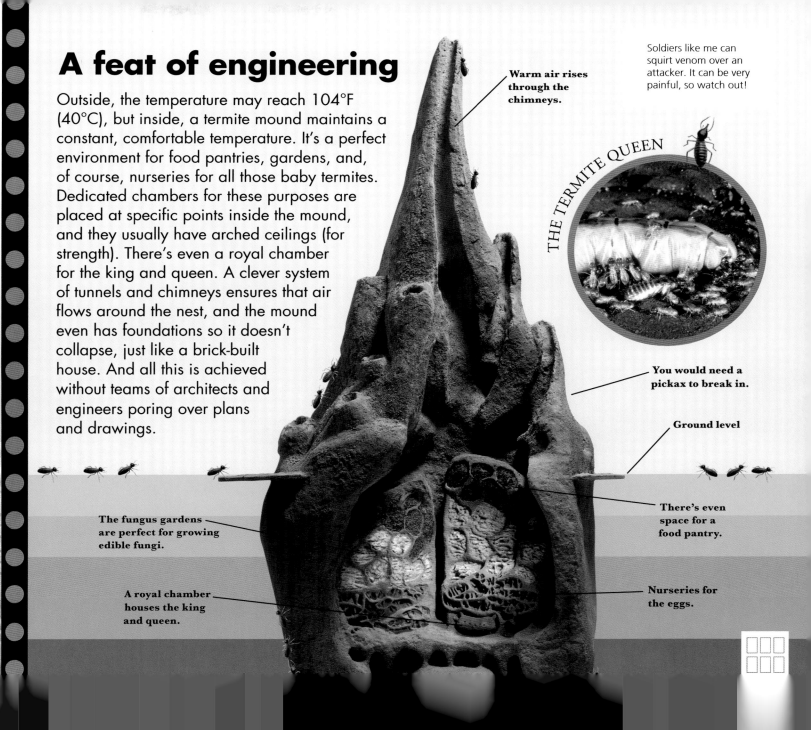

Warm air rises through the chimneys.

Soldiers like me can squirt venom over an attacker. It can be very painful, so watch out!

THE TERMITE QUEEN

You would need a pickax to break in.

Ground level

There's even space for a food pantry.

The fungus gardens are perfect for growing edible fungi.

A royal chamber houses the king and queen.

Nurseries for the eggs.

TOP ten...

1 Gasoline. As a maggot, the petroleum fly of California lives in puddles of crude oil and feeds on other insects that get stuck in the goo. It can submerge itself completely and can swallow oil without a problem—an amazing feat, given that crude oil is poisonous to nearly all living things.

> How do you make a petroleum fly go *"WOOF"*? Set fire to him!

> They may not be cold, but I am!

2 Boiling water. Some shrimp live around spouts of superhot water on the deep-sea floor. Scalding water, heated by underground lava, gushes out of these vents at 660°F (350°C). The shrimp can't stand the heat though—they keep just outside the water spouts and stay in the cool seawater around them.

> Hot dog anyone?

10HHHH

3 Snow and ice. Snow-crawlers are among the few creepy crawlies that can survive at subzero temperatures. They live on snow and scavenge for food. If you pick one up, your body heat will boil it.

4 The sky. Some baby spiders spend their early lives high in the sky, blown around Earth's atmosphere by freezing 300 mph (500 km/h) winds. They stay frozen and thaw as they fall back down.

5 Elephant seal's nose. Possibly the most disgusting place to live on Earth is inside the huge, blubbery nose of an elephant seal, where a certain kind of mite makes its home.

> How about that! Too REVOLTING!

Weird homes!

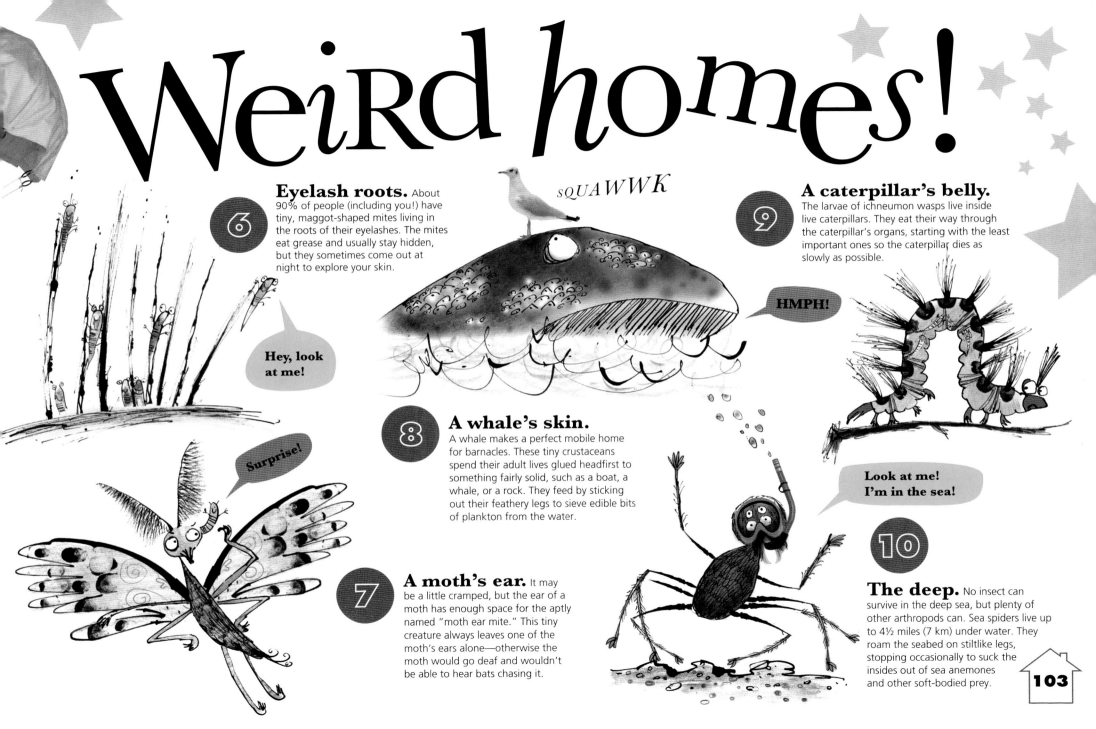

Eyelash roots. About 90% of people (including you!) have tiny, maggot-shaped mites living in the roots of their eyelashes. The mites eat grease and usually stay hidden, but they sometimes come out at night to explore your skin.

6

SQUAWWK

Hey, look at me!

A caterpillar's belly. The larvae of ichneumon wasps live inside live caterpillars. They eat their way through the caterpillar's organs, starting with the least important ones so the caterpillar dies as slowly as possible.

9

HMPH!

A whale's skin. A whale makes a perfect mobile home for barnacles. These tiny crustaceans spend their adult lives glued headfirst to something fairly solid, such as a boat, a whale, or a rock. They feed by sticking out their feathery legs to sieve edible bits of plankton from the water.

8

Surprise!

Look at me! I'm in the sea!

A moth's ear. It may be a little cramped, but the ear of a moth has enough space for the aptly named "moth ear mite." This tiny creature always leaves one of the moth's ears alone—otherwise the moth would go deaf and wouldn't be able to hear bats chasing it.

7

The deep. No insect can survive in the deep sea, but plenty of other arthropods can. Sea spiders live up to 4½ miles (7 km) under water. They roam the seabed on stiltlike legs, stopping occasionally to suck the insides out of sea anemones and other soft-bodied prey.

10

A spiked beast

Colorful *Automeris* caterpillars such as this are found in the lush rain forests of South America. This one was photographed in Peru. Can you think of a reason for its spines?

LARGEr *than* life!

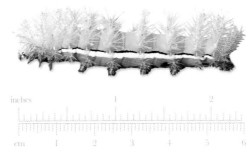

inches   1   2

cm   1   2   3   4   5   6

THIS CATERPILLAR WILL REACH ABOUT 2 ½ IN (6 CM).

Stay back!

The spines are for defense and it's not wise to touch this caterpillar, since they are full of venom. If they pierce your skin, the pain is excruciating. Predators learn very quickly to steer clear.

Arachnophobia

Scared of spiders? Arachnids make up the second biggest branch of the arthropod family tree after insects. They aren't just spiders. Scorpions belong to this class of arthropods, as do ticks and mites, which are the most common arachnids. All these creatures have certain key things in common. They are best known for having eight legs, but they also have four other appendages (called chelicerae and pedipalps) that flank the mouth and work as fangs, feelers, or claws. Unlike insects, arachnids don't have compound eyes or antennae, and their bodies have only two main segments. All are flesh-eaters, and most are ruthlessly efficient killing machines.

Giant house spider

Leg (1 of 8)

Imperial scorpion

Scorpions have huge pedipalps that are used as claws for catching food.

Scorpion
Large claws and sting-tipped tails make scorpions unmistakeable. The most ancient of arachnids, they live only in hot countries and hunt by night. As a rule of thumb, the more menacing a scorpion looks, the less dangerous it is. The deadliest kinds are small with spindly pincers but fat tails packed with venom.

Jumping spider
Bulbous eyes give the tiny jumping spiders the best vision in the spider world. Instead of spinning webs they hunt on foot, carefully sneaking up on victims when they aren't looking.

Opisthosoma (rear segment)

Prosoma (front segment)

Chelicerae (contain fangs)

Spiders have small, armlike pedipalps that are used as feelers to handle food.

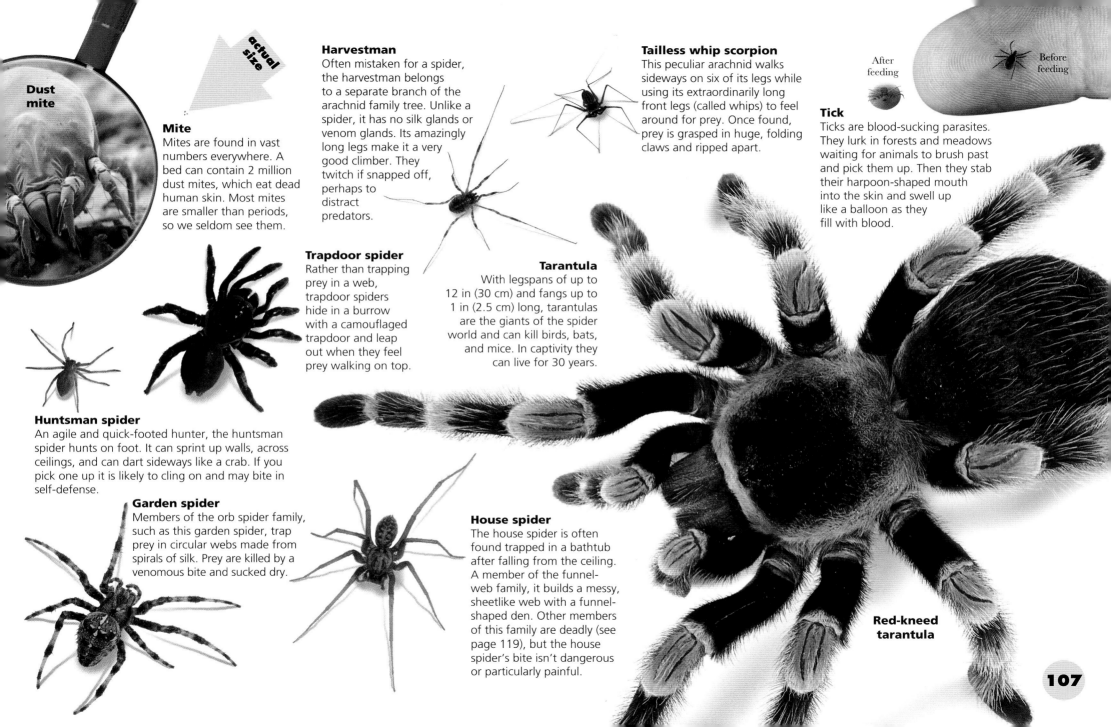

Dust mite

Mite
Mites are found in vast numbers everywhere. A bed can contain 2 million dust mites, which eat dead human skin. Most mites are smaller than periods, so we seldom see them.

actual size

Harvestman
Often mistaken for a spider, the harvestman belongs to a separate branch of the arachnid family tree. Unlike a spider, it has no silk glands or venom glands. Its amazingly long legs make it a very good climber. They twitch if snapped off, perhaps to distract predators.

Trapdoor spider
Rather than trapping prey in a web, trapdoor spiders hide in a burrow with a camouflaged trapdoor and leap out when they feel prey walking on top.

Tailless whip scorpion
This peculiar arachnid walks sideways on six of its legs while using its extraordinarily long front legs (called whips) to feel around for prey. Once found, prey is grasped in huge, folding claws and ripped apart.

After feeding

Before feeding

Tick
Ticks are blood-sucking parasites. They lurk in forests and meadows waiting for animals to brush past and pick them up. Then they stab their harpoon-shaped mouth into the skin and swell up like a balloon as they fill with blood.

Tarantula
With legspans of up to 12 in (30 cm) and fangs up to 1 in (2.5 cm) long, tarantulas are the giants of the spider world and can kill birds, bats, and mice. In captivity they can live for 30 years.

Huntsman spider
An agile and quick-footed hunter, the huntsman spider hunts on foot. It can sprint up walls, across ceilings, and can dart sideways like a crab. If you pick one up it is likely to cling on and may bite in self-defense.

Garden spider
Members of the orb spider family, such as this garden spider, trap prey in circular webs made from spirals of silk. Prey are killed by a venomous bite and sucked dry.

House spider
The house spider is often found trapped in a bathtub after falling from the ceiling. A member of the funnel-web family, it builds a messy, sheetlike web with a funnel-shaped den. Other members of this family are deadly (see page 119), but the house spider's bite isn't dangerous or particularly painful.

Red-kneed tarantula

This magnified length of spider's silk shows just why it stretches so well.

The same silk s t r e t c h e d by five times its length.

The silk has been s t r e t c h e d twenty times its original length.

A spider's web is a feat of **engineering**, and a spiral **orb web**

is built in a particular way and usually at night. It takes the spider about ONE HOUR to build.

Easily damaged by wind and rain, a spider may have to repair its web two or three times a day

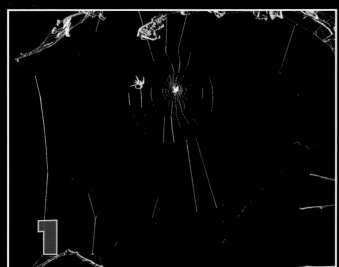

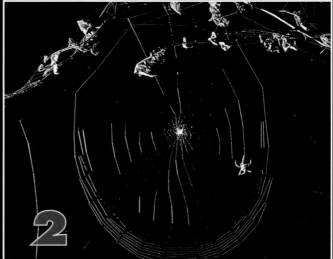

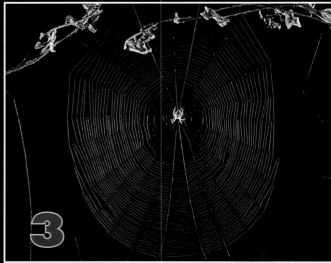

A spider has spun and attached draglines to anchor its new web. These radiate from a central point. It now begins to work around the center.

As the spider works, the threads that touch will stick together, strengthening the web. A web called a spiral orb is beginning to emerge.

The spider now waits at the center of the finished web. It will respond rapidly to any vibrations, since these are caused when an insect is caught.

Web-spinning spiders are born with the skill; no spider is taught how to make a web. Scientists discovered this by isolating baby spiders.

109

Different **types**

of **spiders** build different

types of webs.

Funnel webs
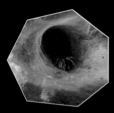
These webs are often built in hidden corners; in cracks in fences or holes in a tree. The spider retreats into the funnel and waits for an insect to get caught before pouncing.

Funnel

Orb webs
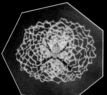
These flat, spiral webs are perhaps the most common of all spider webs. The spider lays draglines and then completes the web by working around and around and around.

Spiral

Tangle webs

These are amazing webs, and they can cover the top of a shrub. The web is a confusion of tangled threads, from which an unfortunate insect has no escape.

Tangle

Sheet webs
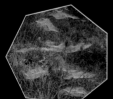
These distinctive webs are so named because the central tangle is a horizontal sheet. Crossed threads above and below the sheet knock flying insects into the sheet.

Sheet

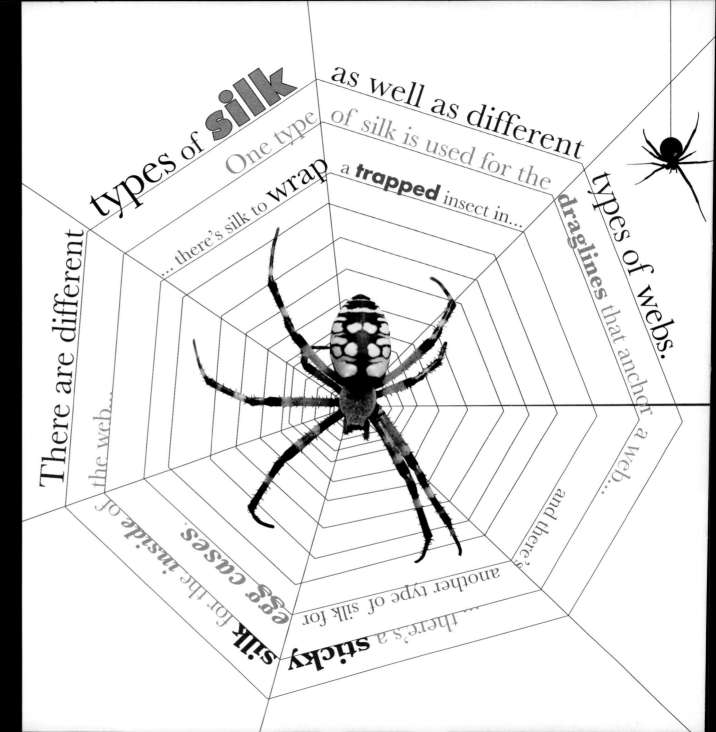

There are different types of **silk** as well as different types of webs.

One type of silk is used for the ...there's silk to wrap a **trapped** insect in...

draglines that anchor a web...

...and there's

the web...

silk for the inside of egg cases.

...there's a **sticky** silk for

another type of silk for

110

webmasters

There is more to a spider's web than meets the eye—weight for weight, the silk strands are some five times stronger than steel. And not only is it strong, it's s-t-r-e-t-c-h-y as well—which makes it ideal for catching insects.

Draglines are produced when a spider starts a web, to anchor it securely.

Stronger than steel

Scientists estimate that if dragline silk (the silk a spider dangles on) could be reproduced with the diameter of a pencil, it would be strong enough to stop a large jet plane in flight.

When a web needs to be repaired the spider will eat the silk and start again.

People have used (and still use) spider silk for all kinds of things, including fishing lures, line, and netting. The largest and strongest web of all is built by the golden orb web spider (though this is not the world's largest spider). This spider's web can cover an area 20 ft (6 m) tall and 7 ft (2 m) wide. Scientists would like to manufacture it, since it could be used for all kinds of things, but it has so far proved impossible.

NOT all spiders build webs

Ground spiders don't, and crab spiders don't. Instead, they hide in leaves and flowers waiting to pounce. Wolf spiders do this, choosing to hunt at night.

Wolf spider

A spider fed coffee will leave huge holes in its web.

111

Male hercules beetle

Big greasy butterfly (male)

Big greasy butterfly (female)

Millar's tiger moth

Jungle nymph stick insect

Shield bug

Common housefly

Ladybug

Dragonfly

Leaf beetle

Hoverfly

Click beetle

Grasshopper

Twin-spotted sphinx moth

Ant

Goliath beetle

Hoverfly

Yellow ladybug

Tarantula hawk wasp

Spot the ODD one out

Are these two pages full of insects? Or has something else crept on?

Violin beetle

Weevil beetle

Chafer beetle

Digger wasp

Stink bug

Giraffe weevil

Earwig

Weevil

Green june beetle

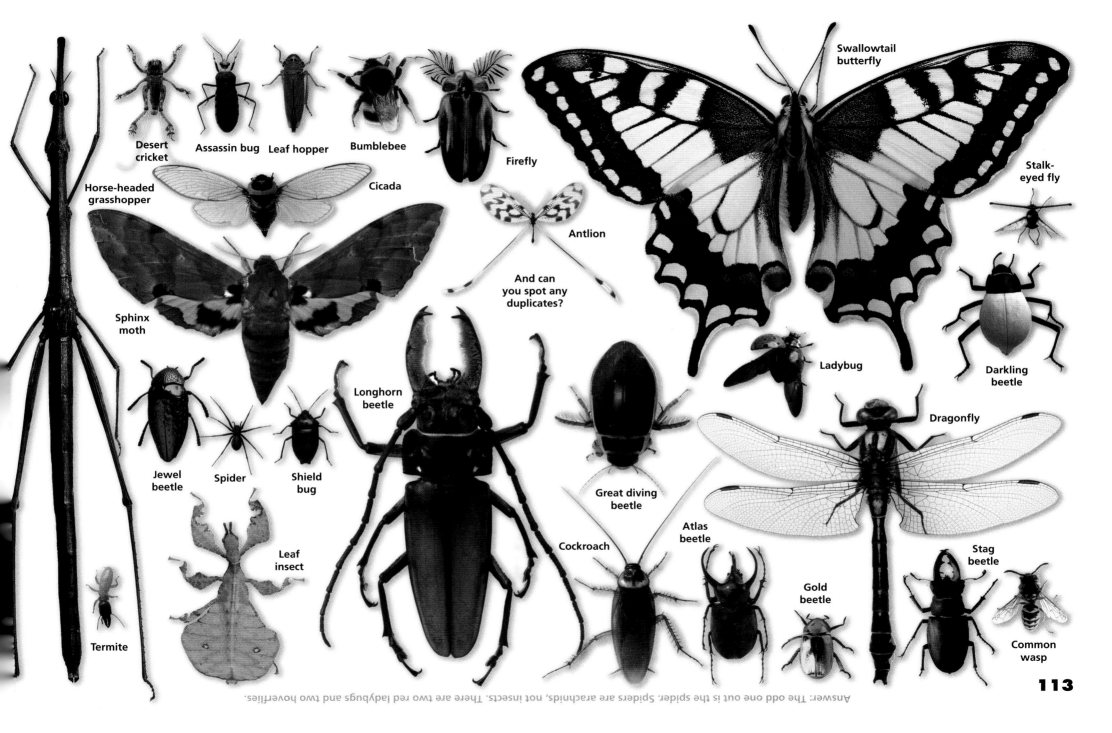

Desert cricket

Assassin bug

Leaf hopper

Bumblebee

Firefly

Swallowtail butterfly

Stalk-eyed fly

Horse-headed grasshopper

Cicada

Antlion

And can you spot any duplicates?

Sphinx moth

Ladybug

Darkling beetle

Longhorn beetle

Dragonfly

Jewel beetle

Spider

Shield bug

Great diving beetle

Leaf insect

Cockroach

Atlas beetle

Gold beetle

Stag beetle

Common wasp

Termite

113

NOW YOU *see* me...

I AM AN IMPERIAL MOTH
(*EACLES IMPERIALIS*) **FROM ECUADOR.**

Centipede

I have at least 15 pairs of legs. My name suggests I have 100 legs (*centi* means "a hundred" in Latin), but most centipedes have far fewer. I am most active at night: it's a good time to hunt!

Centipedes **float**—if they fall into water, they can swim to safety.

Centipedes are **carnivores** that feed on small invertebrates.

Centipedes **run** away if attacked.

Centipedes have **one pair** of legs per segment.

Centipedes are **fast** runners.

Centipedes generally have a **flattened** body.

For its size, a centipede is faster than a cheetah.

Many centipedes have venomous claws located under the head, which are used to kill their prey.

or Millipede?

Feeling threatened, a pill millipede rolls into a tight ball.

Millipedes **sink**. If they fall into water, they will drown.

Most millipedes are **vegetarians**. They feed on decaying vegetation.

Millipedes **roll** into a **ball** if attacked.

Millipedes have **two pairs** of legs per segment.

Millipedes are **slow**-moving.

Millipedes generally have a **rounded** body.

Some millipedes produce a bad smell when they sense a threat.

My name suggests I have 1,000 legs, but no millipede has 1,000 legs; most have around 60, though some have 750. There are a lot more species of millipede than centipede. You'll usually find me burrowing through leaf litter, especially in damp conditions.

117

danger!

Beetle bomb

The bombardier beetle stores explosive chemicals inside two chambers in its abdomen. If you upset this beetle, it will force the two chemicals together so they react and explode. Boiling, caustic chemicals blast out through a swiveling nozzle that the beetle can aim. If the spray hits a small animal in the face, it can blind or kill it.

Suicide mission

Honeybees kill more people than any other venomous animals do. African honeybees are the deadliest. If you step too close to their nest, guard bees release an alarm scent that makes the colony attack as a swarm. They chase relentlessly, delivering hundreds of stings. Each bee dies after stinging, its abdomen ripped open as the stinger pulls out.

118 All these arthropods use **chemical weapons** to **defend** themselves.

chemical warfare

Stinging hairs

In addition to using their venomous fangs for defense, tarantulas can flick a barrage of toxic hairs at attackers. Special "urticating hairs" grow on the abdomen and are flicked off with the legs. The hairs lodge in skin and release chemicals that cause a rash. If they get in your eyes, they can cause excruciating pain.

Stink bomb

Stink bugs have special glands in the thorax that secrete a foul-smelling liquid when the bugs are handled. If you hold one in cupped hands and sniff it, you'll smell the bitter, almondlike odor of cyanide. Some people can't smell cyanide, but the bugs' main enemies—birds— can. The bright colors are also a warning to birds to leave the bug alone.

A sting in the tail

The fat-tailed scorpion of North Africa kills more people than any other scorpion. Its venom contains nerve poisons that spread from the wound to affect the whole body. This is what you can look forward to if you get stung: pain, rapid breathing, weakness, sweating, frothing at the mouth, blurred vision, rolling eyes, vomiting, diarrea, chest pain, seizures, and death.

Kiss of death

The Sydney funnel-web spider is one of the few spiders whose bite can kill a human, though deaths are rare. It bites aggressively and repeatedly, and its fangs can pierce a fingernail or puncture a shoe. The venom contains a cocktail of nerve poisons that can cause unbearable pain, twitching, vomiting, coma, and death.

Prickly peril

Never touch a spiked or hairy caterpillar. The spikes and hairs are designed to break into needle-sharp fragments that pierce your skin and inject a pain-inducing venom. Caterpillars can also steal chemical weapons from plants. They feed on poisonous plants and store the toxic chemicals in their bodies for protection.

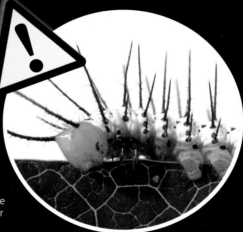

Take the pain

The bullet ant of Central America has the most painful sting of any insect. The searing pain lasts 24 hours and is said to be like a bullet piercing the body. Rain-forest tribes use the ants in a ceremony of manhood. Boys wear a woven sleeve in which the ants are trapped, and must endure dozens of stings to prove their courage.

 **DEADLY** **CORROSIVE** ! **IRRITATING**

"Doctor Arthropod!"

REMOVE WARTS ╋ STITCH WOUNDS ╋ CLEAN ULCERS

Wart-biter bush cricket
(*Decticus verrucivorus*)

People in Europe once used this large cricket to remove warts. They placed the cricket on a finger and then let it wander up to the wart and eat it. As the cricket feeds, it produces a brown, salivalike substance that was thought to kill the infected cells. Entomologists who have tried it say it does appear to work... but it hurts like crazy!

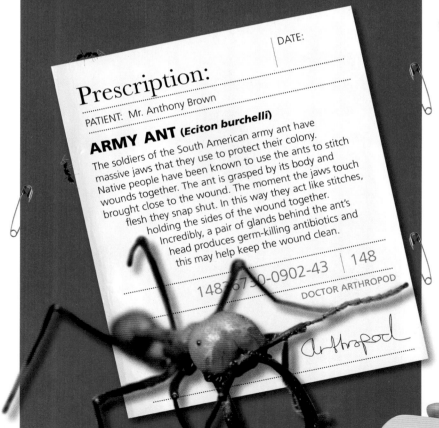

Prescription:

PATIENT: Mr. Anthony Brown

ARMY ANT (*Eciton burchelli*)
The soldiers of the South American army ant have massive jaws that they use to protect their colony. Native people have been known to use the ants to stitch wounds together. The ant is grasped by its body and brought close to the wound. The moment the jaws touch flesh they snap shut. In this way they act like stitches, holding the sides of the wound together. Incredibly, a pair of glands behind the ant's head produces germ-killing antibiotics and this may help keep the wound clean.

14826750-0902-43 | 148

DOCTOR ARTHROPOD

DATE:

Medical maggots at work

BLOWFLY (*Lucilius*)
Certain blowfly larvae eat only infected flesh. If you put them in an open wound, they also produce a secretion that kills germs. However, it's vital to use the correct species. Get it wrong and the maggots bore into living flesh and then work their way up to toward the head.

Arthropods are much more likely to give you a **disease** than to *cure* you, but there are just A FEW creepy crawlies that might help if you're sick...

BANDAGE INJURIES ✛ MAKE LOVE POTIONS ✛ DRAIN BLOOD

House spider
(*Agalena*)

The thick webs spun by the house spider have been used as bandages to stop bleeding. As spiders regularly catch flies, and flies carry many different types of disease, this is one treatment that should be used only in emergencies.

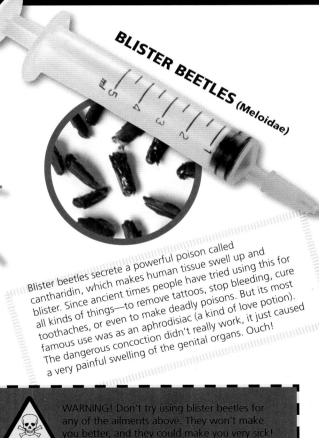

BLISTER BEETLES (Meloidae)

Blister beetles secrete a powerful poison called cantharidin, which makes human tissue swell up and blister. Since ancient times people have tried using this for all kinds of things—to remove tattoos, stop bleeding, cure toothaches, or even to make deadly poisons. But its most famous use was as an aphrodisiac (a kind of love potion). The dangerous concoction didn't really work, it just caused a very painful swelling of the genital organs. Ouch!

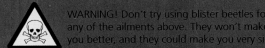

⚠ WARNING! Don't try using blister beetles for any of the ailments above. They won't make you better, and they could make you very sick!

Leeches
(*Hirudo medicinalis*)

The medicinal leech is not an arthropod but a bloodsucking worm. Its saliva contains substances that help blood to flow and stop it from clotting. This makes leeches handy in medical procedures where doctors need to keep a person's blood flowing freely.

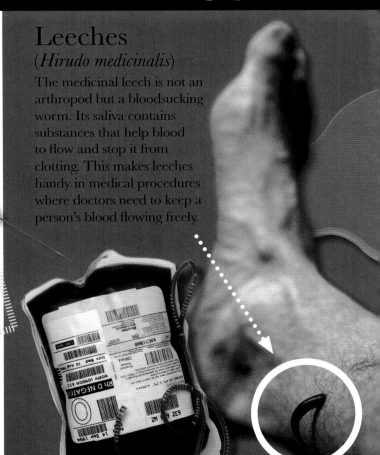

1 Cockroaches can live if their **heads** are *removed*.

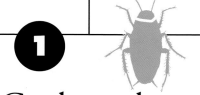

2 **Male** spiders are always **eaten** by the female.

3 Some **spiders** lay their eggs *in a person's skin.* A few weeks later, hundreds of baby spiders **burst** out.

4 **Daddy longlegs** have the most deadly venom of all arachnids, but their fangs are too small to bite humans.

true...

6 True. Count how many times the cricket chirps in 15 seconds, add 40, and the answer is the temperature in degrees Fahrenheit.

7 False-ish. Just like us, they would be killed by the blast and heat. However, because they live underground for most of their lives, they might be shielded from much of the damage. Although their exoskeletons are slightly better at reflecting radiation than our skin is, and their breathing system is less likely to take in radioactive dust, they fall victim to radiation poisoning just as surely as us. The one true advantage they have, and this applies to cockroaches even more, is their reproductive rate. The more offspring they have, the greater the chance that some will survive.

8 False. They already have.

9 True. The parasitic mermithid worms can alter the behavior of their host and force it to seek out puddles of water and drown itself. The worms then burst out of the dead body. The grasshopper can fight back if it's quick enough: early stages of infection can be cured by basking. The grasshopper climbs out in the open at midday and allows its body temperature to reach 104°F (40°C). Though close to fatal for the grasshopper, the high temperature kills the worms.

5

 Mayflies only **live** for one day.

6

 Grasshoppers have their **brains** taken over by massive worms and are forced to *commit suicide*.

7

Scorpions can survive a **nuclear bomb**.

8

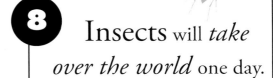 Insects will *take over the world* one day.

9

 A cricket's song can tell you what the **temperature** is.

or false?

5. False. Although the adult stage can last as little as an hour, the mayfly has spent at least one year (and possibly as long as seven years) as an aquatic nymph. Many adult insects have short lives, especially the males. Often this is because neither sex has a mouth, and it's usually the males that have to seek out the females, exhausting their reserves of stored energy as they do so.

4. False. None of the various arthropods known as daddy longlegs have deadly venom.

3. False. No spider or close relative of spiders lays eggs in this way.

2. False. Most male spiders are far too careful to get eaten—their goal is to mate with as many females as they can. Nevertheless, they do run the risk of falling victim to their partner's predatory instincts. And in one Southeast Asian species, death is guaranteed: the male cannot hold on to the dangling female unless she skewers him with her fangs.

1. True. However, they die after 4–7 days because they are unable to eat or drink and therefore dehydrate and starve very quickly.

Friend OR

WARNING! Wasps can turn aggressive at the end of the year!

Wasps might have a nasty sting, but they are efficient predators and kill huge numbers of pests, such as caterpillars. Definitely friends.

Honeybees give us honey and wax, and they also carry pollen from flower to flower, helping crops to produce fruit and seeds. So they are mostly friends... except the dreaded African variety, which isn't very friendly at all.

Ladybugs are also friendly predators. They prey on the tiny greenflies that infest garden plants. Some people buy ladybugs and release them in greenhouses to control pests.

Don't panic! I'm gonna get that pesky fly!

Spiders kill billions of pests and disease-carrying insects, especially flies, and they never lay a fang on our plants or buildings.

Bumblebees are great pollinators, dutifully buzzing from flower to flower and so helping plants to fruit. They are especially good at pollinating greenhouse plants like tomatos.

I'm a foe because I spread disease, but I can also be a friend and help recycle things. See page 84 to find out how!

FOE?

Many people think **insects** and **spiders** are just *pests* that infest our homes and gardens. In fact, a lot of them actually help us. So who are our **friends** and who are our **foes?**

Carpenter ants dig hollows in wood for their nests, and they don't care whether the wood is part of a tree or an important part of your home. At night they sneak out to raid your kitchen for sweet or greasy foods.

Greenflies suck the sap out of all kinds of plants and multiply at a phenomenal rate by giving birth to clones without having to mate. They also squirt out sugary excrement that causes mold.

Fee, fie, **foe**, fum...

Cabbage white butterflies may be pretty, but their caterpillars aren't popular with gardeners. They eat nearly the all same vegetables as us: cauliflowers, cabbages, sprouts, broccoli, radishes, kale, mustard...

Flour beetles find their way into kitchen cupboards and feast on all kinds of dried food, from flour and pasta to crackers and powdered milk. Most definitely foes!

Termites don't just burrow into the lumber of houses—they eat them. They do it all out of sight, so they can totally wreck a house before you discover them.

Colorado beetles once lived only in the Rocky Mountains, but they have now spread across the world as a pest of potato plants. The larvae devour the leaves and ruin the crop.

Hmmm, moldy old flour—my favorite!

125

What is the **deadliest** animal in the **world?**

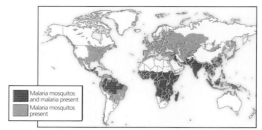

Malaria used to be a global disease. The types of mosquito that can spread the malaria germs are found nearly everywhere, except deserts and very cold places. In the 20th century, many countries succeeded in wiping out the germs (though not the mosquitos). However, malaria is still common in tropical countries, as are the other mosquito-borne diseases listed below.

Malaria mosquitos and malaria present
Malaria mosquitos present

Meet the humble female mosquito, cause of nearly half of all human deaths in history. As she drives her piercing mouthparts deep into your skin to suck your blood, she can also inject microscopic germs that cause a fatal disease. Malaria is the most common—it kills about 2 million people a year. But it's not the only one. Travel in a malaria zone and you run the risk of getting any of the nasty diseases below.

Before supper...

... after supper

Female mosquitos suck human blood so that they can make eggs. Males don't bite and are so small and insignificant that you've probably never seen one. You're most likely to get bitten in the evening when the air is still—mosquitos rest during daylight and they can't stand moving air. As the female drinks, her abdomen swells up with blood and turns red. Her saliva contains a painkiller so you don't feel the bite... until it's too late.

What *mosquitos* can do for you

DENGUE FEVER causes a rash of red spots on your skin and terrible pains in your joints and bones.
YELLOW FEVER turns your vomit black and your skin yellow. Then you go into a coma and die.
WEST NILE VIRUS spreads through your blood into your brain, which then swells up and kills you.
MALARIA produces a raging fever that flares up repeatedly every two or three days. Often fatal.
ELEPHANTIASIS makes your legs swell up like elephants' legs because of tiny worms, spread by mosquitos, that burrow into your skin.

Malaria germs breed inside **red blood cells** (shown here magnified).

In 1790, **10%** of Philadelphia's population was wiped out...

Malaria can kill you in **1 day** or can stay hidden in your body for **30 years.**

... in a single summer by **yellow fever.**

1 in **17** of all people alive today will die because of a mosquito bite.

500 million people catch malaria every year.

1 in **5** people who catch the most severe form of malaria die.

22,000 French workers died building the Panama Canal because of **malaria** and **yellow fever.**

Every **12** seconds a child dies of **malaria.**

More than **half** of Napoleon's army was killed by yellow fever when he invaded Haiti in 1802.

Malaria doesn't just make humans sick—it makes mosquitos sick too.

Arthropods at risk—who's

Many arthropods are listed as **endangered species,** on a scale from VULNERABLE through endangered to EXTINCT.

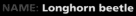

NAME: **Longhorn beetle**
Macrodontia cervicornis
STATUS: vulnerable
One species among many victims of the destruction of rain forests, these South American beetles are also hunted by collectors to sell for display.

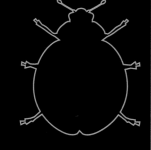

NAME: **7-spot ladybug**
Coccinella septempunctata
STATUS: common—but for how much longer?
A common sight in British gardens and meadows, these beetles are being edged out by the invasion of non-native harlequin ladybugs, which compete for food—and then eat the 7-spots when the aphids run out.

NAME: **Coconut crab**
Birgus latro
STATUS: unknown
While coconut crabs thrive on some of the islands in the Pacific and Indian Oceans, on the more populated ones they are being overharvested as a prized delicacy.

NAME: **Raft spider**
Dolomedes plantarius
STATUS: vulnerable
This European spider lives in lowland wetlands—a habitat that is under threat from pollution and evaporation due to global warming.

NAME: **St. Helena earwig**
Labidura herculeana
STATUS: critically endangered
Not seen alive since 1967, the possibly extinct giant earwig is thought to have been wiped out by non-native predators, especially the giant centipede.

on the missing list?

The causes include **habitat loss**, *harvesting*, and being **eaten** by introduced species—which can all be traced back to PEOPLE.

NAME: Fregate Beetle
Polposipus herculeanus
STATUS: critically endangered
Found only on Fregate Island in the Seychelles, these beetles not only face being eaten by non-native predators, but are also being made homeless by a fungus that is killing off the trees they live in.

NAME: Giant weta
Deinacrida spp
STATUS: vulnerable
These cricket-type insects that live on islands off the New Zealand mainland are eaten by non-native predators, including cats, rats, and hedgehogs.

NAME: Queen Alexandra's birdwing *Ornithoptera alexandrae*
STATUS: endangered
The birdwing feeds on only one species of plant, which is under threat of rain forest destruction in Papua New Guinea. Collectors also hunt the birdwing, the world's largest and rarest butterfly.

NAME: Wallace's giant bee *Megachile pluto*
STATUS: unknown
Once thought to be extinct, these Indonesian bees make their homes inside termite nests, which is why they are almost never seen—despite being the world's largest bees.

NAME: Red barbed ant
Formica rufibarbis
STATUS: endangered
Always rare, this British ant faces more habitat loss as fields are built on. Its relative the slave-making ant is another threat—it destroys nests by stealing larvae to raise as slaves.

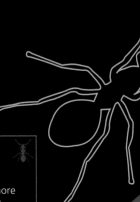

HAVE WE SEEN THE LAST OF THEM?

129

WORKING WITH BUGS

Getting to the honey can be quite a stretch.

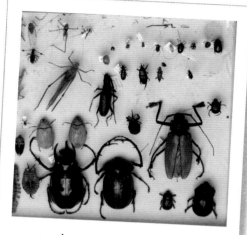

That's the latest collection laid out. Now to name them...

Job satisfaction is seeing people enjoy my displays.

It's a dirty job but someone has to do it!

BEEKEEPER

Protective clothing is usually pale-colored and smooth—the opposite of the dark fur of the bees' natural predators, such as bears.

It's summertime in the northern hemisphere, and beekeepers reap their reward for nine months of caring for their colonies and maintaining hives: it's honey collection time. Beekeepers don protective veils and hats before approaching the hive—bees are attracted to human breath and can inflict painful stings on the face.

TAXONOMIST

Of the estimated 30 million types of living organisms on Earth, taxonomists have identified and named just six percent (1.2 million) of them.

Before taxonomists can get on with their job of identifying and naming insects, the specimens need to be collected. For example, insects living high up in a forest canopy will be sprayed with pesticide so they fall onto a sheet below. Species may be studied with electron microscopes that magnify the original by up to 200,000 times.

MUSEUM CURATOR

Curators don't just display their exhibits, they also keep them safe. This is vital when a museum may have the only specimen in existence.

Ever wondered who makes the displays in museums? It's the job of a curator. These highly qualified specialists acquire the exhibits for display, and work out how best to show them and write the information that goes with them. Sometimes exhibits need to be researched to check their authenticity—the curator arranges that too.

PEST EXTERMINATOR

Working both indoors and out, this varied job includes removing wasps' nests from houses and cleaning cockroaches from restaurant kitchens.

Decked out in protective overalls, gloves, face mask, and goggles, the exterminator delivers a powerful blast of chemical pesticide to kill bugs. The job uses dangerous chemicals and tools in the quest to keep people (and plants) disease-free. It isn't always easy either, involving digging, clearing trees, and climbing ladders to get to the pests.

WHO WOULD WANT TO DO *THAT*?

It's amazing what a dead specimen can reveal...

Getting down to business—and entertaining the crowd.

Carefully does it, I don't want to drop the insect trap.

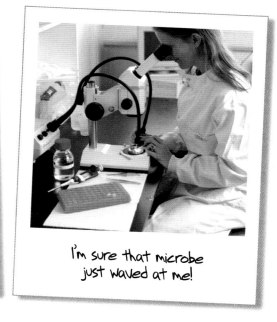

I'm sure that microbe just waved at me!

FORENSIC ENTOMOLOGIST

Forensic entomologists may be called to a scene of crime to gather evidence, or may be sent samples by a police forensic scientist.

Forensic entomologists are crime detectives. In the lab, they cross-examine insects to give a wide range of information. For example, flies and maggots can reveal how long a corpse has been dead; and wasp remains on a car windshield might show the path a car was taking when it crashed.

ZOOKEEPER

Frequently working into the night and on the weekends, being a professional zookeeper and tending to animals is a bit like being a parent!

If you thought owning a pet was a lot of work, zookeepers have a far busier time! The keeper looks after everything, from designing the cage and keeping it clean, to feeding the animal and noticing when it might not be feeling well. They talk to zoo visitors, work with vets, and share knowledge with other experts to conserve species.

CONSERVATIONIST

Often called on to help with regeneration programs, conservationists can be the last hope for species at threat from extinction.

The conservationist has a dual role of research and PR. They identify species under threat—perhaps developers want to put offices in a field, but it's the only home in the country of a rare species of butterfly. It's the conservationists who devise the campaign to change the construction plans, and raise awareness of the species at the same time.

RESEARCH SCIENTIST

Patience is vital: not only do results take time to come through, but when experiments don't work, they may be repeated again and again.

Research scientists spend not even half their time actually performing experiments—there's a lot of analysis and writing reports to go with it. Practical experiments might include dissection and breaking down animal tissue to get to the DNA, in order to study the evolution of the animal.

131

Insect inspired

Nicknamed **"The Gherkin"** because of its conical shape, the design of 30 St. Mary Axe in London is based on **termite mounds**. The building has energy-efficient ventilation shafts just like the air vents made by termites.

THE BEATLES
JOHN, PAUL, GEORGE, AND RINGO

Vespa scooters are named after their engines. The noise sounds just like a *vespa*—Italian for **"wasp."**

Insects might be small, but their namesakes can be big! **The Beatles** are one of the most successful rock groups of all time. Some of their musical inspiration came from earlier groups such as **Buddy Holly and the Crickets**.

Bookworms, watch out! There are lots of reading bugs to catch, from Eric Carle's classic *The Very Hungry Caterpillar* to **Ladybird books**, which have been inhabiting shelves for nearly 100 years.

Ancient Egyptians revered **scarab beetles** for their apparent creation from nothing. (Actually, they are born underground and crawl to the surface.) Centuries-old amulets are often copied in modern **jewelry**.

ART and science often *imitate* **nature.** From insect **movement** to *names* and **homes**, can you spot the small **beginnings** behind these DESIGNS?

Cicely Mary Barker's **Flower Fairies** might be inspired by different flowers, but the fairies themselves show distinctly butterflylike natures, such as the shape of their wings and their habit of zipping around flowers.

How hygienic are **flies**? This rather oversized specimen decorates a balcony at the London School of Hygiene and Tropical Medicine. At least the scientists can be sure the metal insect isn't carrying any **diseases**!

The flight of the bumble bee

The **VW Beetle** car is obviously named for its shape, and most countries call it their local equivalent of "beetle." But some just have to be different: in Bolivia it's a turtle (*Peta*) and in Indonesia it's a frog (*Kodok*).

Crawling up buildings... spinning webs... saving the world? Well, **Spiderman** might not get *all* his talents from our **arachnid** friends.

The London **Wasps** are a rugby union club—but what came first, their name or their striped shirts? It was in fact the name, which dates back to 1867. In those days it was fashionable to call teams after all kinds of animals.

RECORD BREAKERS

 MIGRATION Some animals embark on long journeys, called migrations, to find new homes. Arthropods can migrate thousands of miles by riding on the wind. The desert locust (*Schistocerca gregaria*) of Africa regularly travels vast distances in wind-blown swarms across the Sahara Desert as it searches for food. In 1988, a swarm flew all the way across the Atlantic Ocean by riding on powerful tropical winds that later generated a hurricane. The locusts landed in the South American countries of Surinam and Guyana and on the Virgin Islands.

longest fastest tallest highest loudest smallest

Longest INSECT

Pharnacia kirbiyi, a stick insect from jungles in Borneo, is a staggering 22 in (55 cm) long—about the same as the width of this book when open.

Fastest on land

The American cockroach is the official holder of this record, with a top speed of 3½ mph (5.4 km/h). But scientific reports suggest an Australian tiger beetle may be capable of 5½ mph (8.96 km/h)—nearly twice as fast.

Tallest HOME

African termite mounds, at up to 42 ft (13 m) tall, are the tallest buildings made by any non-human animal. If we made buildings as big in proportion to our bodies, they would be 3 miles (4.5 km) tall.

Best JUMPER

The cat flea is the champion high-jumper of the insect world, capable of reaching 13 in (34 cm) high, which is 140 times a flea's height and therefore equivalent to a human leaping on to a seven-story building in a single bound.

Largest BUTTERFLY

Queen Alexandra's birdwing of Papua New Guinea is the biggest butterfly, with a wingspan of 11 in (28 cm). The biggest moth is the Hercules moth of Australia, which also has a 11 in (28 cm) wingspan.

Philip McCabe stood for over 2 hours covered in 60 lb (27 kg) of bees and was stung only seven times.

 **MOST BABIES** Social insects have more babies than any other arthropods. A queen honeybee lays 200,000 eggs a year and lives for 4 years, so she can produce 800,000 offspring in her life. But the record holder is the queen termite. Laying eggs at average rate of 21 a minute, she produces 30,000 eggs a day. She lives for about 10 years, during which time she can have 100 million offspring.

laziest youngest oldest smallest loudest highest

Shortest LIFE

Mayflies have the shortest adult lives of insects, lasting only a day or so. Adult females of the species *Dolania americana* live for only 5 minutes. Aphids have the shortest generation time—they can give birth 5 days after being born.

Smallest SPIDER

Patu marplesi of Samoa is the world's smallest spider, at only 0.017 in (0.43 mm) long. However, other arachnids, such as mites, are smaller. The smallest insect is a wingless wasp 0.005 in (0.14 mm) long.

LONGEST hibernation

Yucca moths have been known to spend 19 years hibernating as pupas before emerging as adult moths. Many insects are capable of entering a state of hibernation (actually called diapause) in order to avoid cold or dry weather.

LARGEST WEB

Golden orb web spiders build silk webs 10 ft (3 m) wide. They sometimes span rivers and are strong enough to catch small birds.

oldest youngest laziest smelliest

Fastest BUG

Hawkmoths are joint holders of the world record for fastest flying insect, along with horseflies, botflies, and certain butterflies. Their top speed is 24 mph (39 km/h).

FASTEST wing beat

Forcipomyia—a kind of midge—can beat its wings 1,046 times a second. The wings are powered by the fastest muscles known to exist.

LOUDEST insect

Male cicadas can sing at volumes of up to 109 decibels, which is almost as loud as a jackhammer. The songs are audible from ¼ mile (0.5 km) away.

Biggest BEE BEARD

Philip McCabe of Ireland risked being stung to death when he covered himself with 200,000 honey bees in June 2005 in an attempt to beat the world record for "largest bee beard." The current record is 350,000 bees, held by Mark Biancaniello of California.

LONGEST LIFE

Wood-boring beetles probably have the longest life of any insect. They can survive as larvae inside wood for 50 years before emerging as adults. Queen ants probably have the longest adult lives of insects, surviving for up to 30 years as head of their colony.

fastest longest

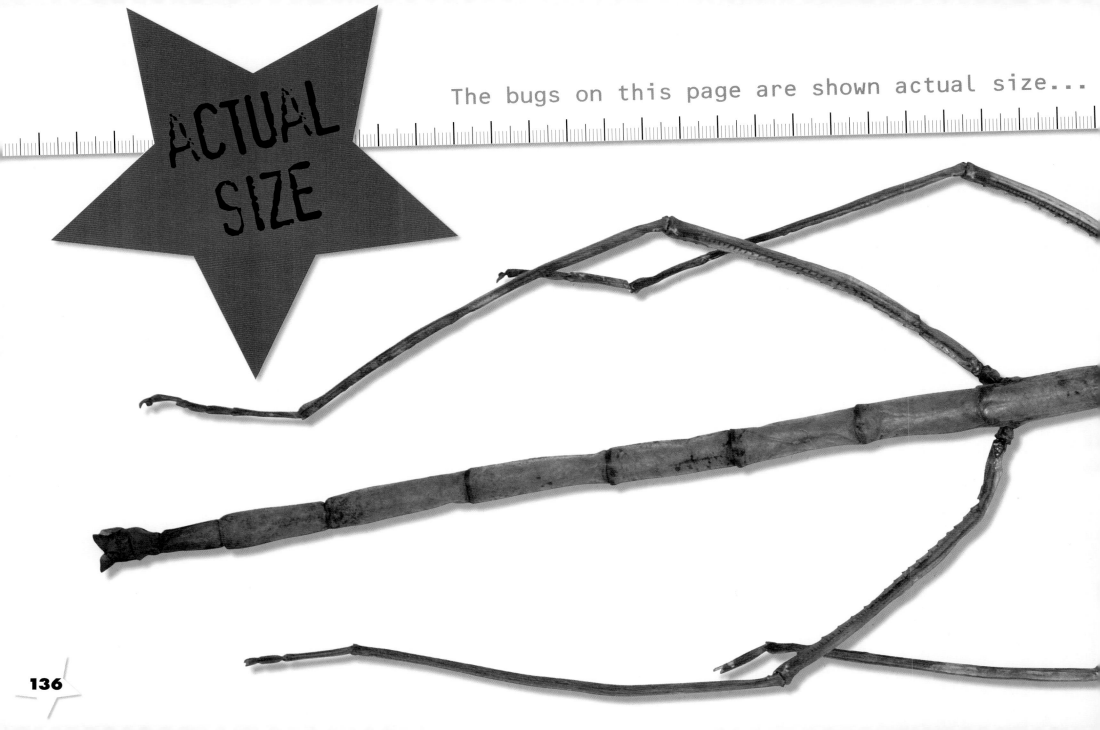

ACTUAL SIZE

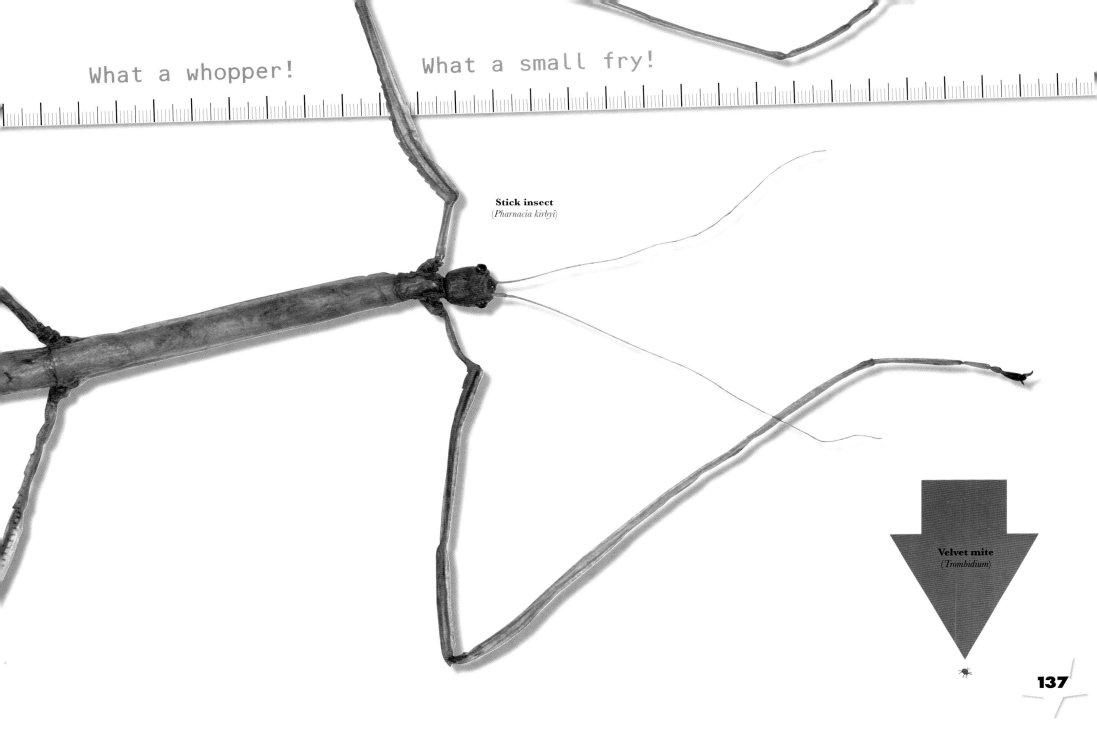

What a whopper!   What a small fry!

Stick insect
(*Pharnacia kirbyi*)

Velvet mite
(*Trombidium*)

137

GLOSSARY

Abdomen the part of an animal's body that contains digestive and reproductive organs. An insect's abdomen is at the rear of the body.

Antennae (feelers) long sensory organs on the head of an arthropod. They feel, taste, and smell objects, as well as sensing vibrations.

Arachnid a member of the class Arachnida, a particular branch of the arthropod family tree. Arachnids have eight legs and include spiders, scorpions, ticks, and mites.

Arthropod an animal with a jointed external skeleton.

Camouflage patterns or colors that help an animal blend in with its background and hide from enemies.

Rhinoceros beetle grub
(*Oryctes centaurus*)

Caterpillar the wingless larva of a butterfly or moth.

Chrysalis the pupa of a butterfly. Chysalises have a hard outer case for protection.

Cocoon the protective silk case around the pupa of a moth.

Colony a large group of animals living close together. Social insects such as bees and ants live in colonies.

Compound eye an eye made up of hundreds of tiny units, each of which makes a separate image.

Crustacean a member of the superclass Crustacea, a particular branch of the arthropod family tree. Most crustaceans live in water. Crabs, shrimp, lobsters, and woodlice are crustaceans.

Digestive organs the parts of the body that break down food so that it can be absorbed.

Entomology the scientific study of insects.

Exoskeleton the outer skeleton (cuticle) of an arthropod.

Fang a long, sharp tooth.

Gill an organ used to breathe underwater.

Grub the larva (immature form) of a beetle, wasp, or bee.

Haltere one of a pair of drumstick-shaped structures on a fly's body that beat with the wings to aid balance.

Hive a manmade structure built to house a bee colony.

Insect a member of the class Insecta, a particular branch of the arthropod family tree. Insects have three main body parts and six legs.

Invertebrate An animal without a backbone. All arthropods are invertebrates, as are worms, snails, slugs, and many sea creatures.

Larva an immature form of an insect. Larvae look very different from the adults. Caterpillars are the larvae of butterflies.

Metamorphosis the dramatic change that occurs when a larva (an immature insect) turns into an adult. Caterpillars metamorphose when they change into butterflies.

Migration a long journey by an animal to find a new place to live. Some animals migrate regularly every year.

Molting the shedding of an arthropod's exoskeleton. Arthropods have to molt in order to grow.

Nectar a sugary liquid made by flowers to attract pollinating insects.

Nymph an immature form of an insect that looks similar to the adult. Nymphs grow into adults by molting several times.

Parasite a small organism that lives on or inside the body of a bigger organism, feeding on it while it is still alive.

Pedipalps a pair of small armlike appendages on the head of an arachnid, on each side of the mouth.

Pollen a powdery substance, made in flowers, that contains male sex cells. When pollen is transferred to the female part of a flower, the flower can produce a seed or fruit.

Pollination the transfer of pollen from male organs in flowers to female organs. Pollination is a very important stage in the reproduction of plants.

Predator an animal that kills and eats other animals.

Prey an animal that is killed and eaten by a predator.

Proboscis a long, flexible snout or mouthpart. A butterfly uses a proboscis (also called a tongue) to suck nectar from flowers.

Pupa the resting stage in the life cycle of an insect, during which a larva is tranformed into an adult by the process of metamorphosis.

Sap a liquid that transports nutrients around plants.

Silk a tough, stretchy fiber produced by spiders to make webs or by moth caterpillars to make cocoons.

Solitary alone.

Species a type of organism. The members of a species can breed with each other but not with other species.

Spiracle a hole in the exoskeleton of an arthropod that lets air circulate through the body.

Thorax the central body part of an insect, between the head and abdomen.

Venom a poisonous substance in an animal's bite or sting.

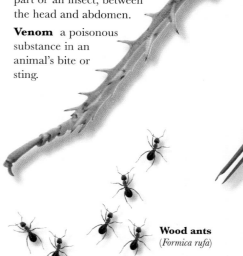

Wood ants
(*Formica rufa*)

138

Housefly
(*Musca domestica*)

Giant weta
(*Deinacrida rugosa*)

CREDITS

Longhorn beetle
(*Titanus giganteus*)

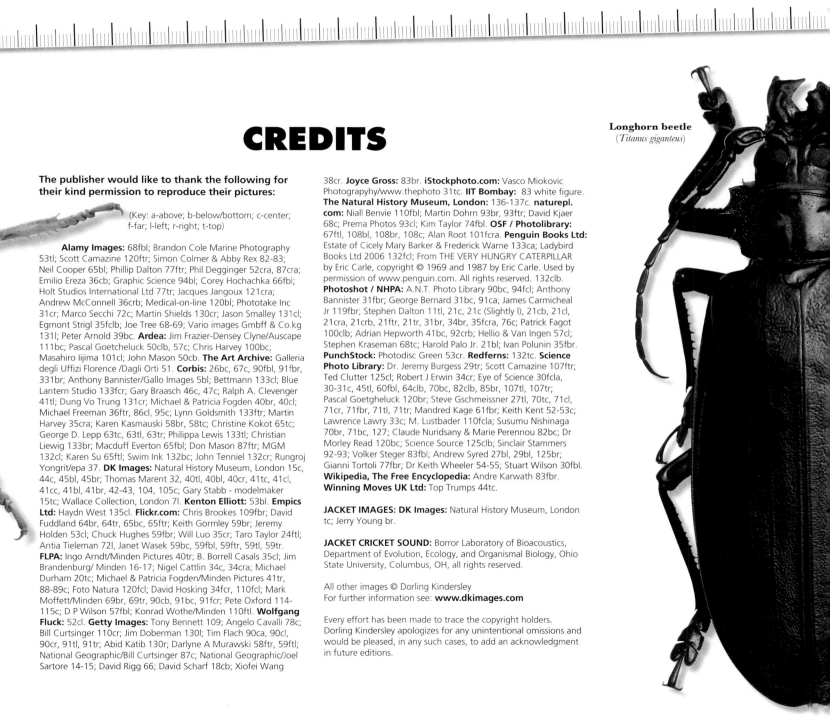

index